W9-AXA-526

VICTORY

FOR

KIDS

The Cleveland School Voucher Case

DAVID L. BRENNAN

With Malcolm Baroway
Foreword by David Zanotti

NEW MILLENNIUM PRESS
Beverly Hills

Copyright © 2002 David Brennan

Victory for Kids
The Cleveland Voucher Case

All rights reserved. No part of this book may be produced or transmitted in any form or by any means, electronic or mechanical, including photocopying, recording or by any information storage retrieval system without permission in writing from the publisher.

Text Design by Kerry DeAngelis, KL Design

ISBN: 1-893224-76-7

New Millennium Press
301 North Canon Drive
Suite 214
Beverly Hills, CA 90210

10 9 8 7 6 5 4 3 2 1

Malcolm Baroway writes, edits, and paints in oils at his home in Columbus, Ohio. He has directed the public relations programs of both the University of Michigan and The Ohio State University.

David Zanotti is president of the non-partisan statewide public policy organizations, the Ohio Roundtable and the Ohio Freedom Forum, headquartered in Strongsville, Ohio. He also chairs the School Choice Committee, comprised of business and community leaders, educators, ministers, and elected officials dedicated to expand educational opportunity for children through parental choice.

This book is a saga in two parts. The prologue and first 14 chapters were written as the United States Supreme Court was deciding the Cleveland School Voucher Case. The final five chapters were written soon after the favorable decision was rendered. In total, they present the story of a case whose outcome may prove as important to the nation as any in its history.

Dedication

This book is dedicated to Lydia Harris, a dear friend. Lydia was my inspiration when she was principal of St. Adalbert School, who set me off on the journey to establish voucher schools that would replicate what she was accomplishing at St. Adalbert. Without her, there would have been no Cleveland voucher plan, no U.S. Supreme Court case, and no court decision. I am deeply indebted to you, Lydia.

And to John Morris, the first Principal of Hope Central Academy, the President and CEO of White Hat Management, and a very dear friend.

"All great ideas go through three stages: In the first stage, they are ridiculed. In the second stage, they are strongly opposed. In the third stage, they are considered to be self-evident."

Arthur Schopenhauer, German Philosopher
(1788-1860)

Theme of the Work

"The fundamental theory of liberty upon which all governments in this Union repose excludes any general power of the state to standardize its children by forcing them to accept instruction from public teachers only. The child is not the mere creature of the State."

The United States Supreme Court
Pierce v. Society of Sisters, 1925
(Unanimous decision)

Contents

Prologue

March 2002

How often in history has one person come forward to lead a major reform initiative all the way to the United States Supreme Court? How often have so many people slept outside that historic building in the middle of winter hoping for the chance to get inside and hear the debate? One marshal told me he had seen such a crowd only one time since *Roe v. Wade*: The time the Court decided the 2000 presidential election.

David Brennan and his wife, Ann, were invited to take a first-row seat. They belonged there. So did Jo Ann Davidson, former Speaker of the Ohio House, and Lisa Sadler, the trial judge from Franklin County, who first heard the case. Five or six seats down sat Ted Kennedy. The clock swept past 10:00; the buzzer sounded. The justices strode through a red curtain and the drama began.

I have sat through tons of trials and hearings in my career in public policy, too many to count. Seldom have I seen judges with such intense knowledge of a case. For 80 straight minutes the Court was fully engaged, attacking with questions, challenging each

1

other, demanding more details. They knew the score in the Cleveland public school system. They knew transportation issues, student enrollment, per pupil spending. They challenged our legal team on the real meanings of the Ohio law. Our team, including Judi French, chief state solicitor, Dave Young, and Ted Olson, lawyer for the President of the United States, was more than ready to defend the plan that came from the heartland.

I'm watching Ted Olson in action and thinking to myself, "I remember when we debated that very same question in Dave Brennan's office nearly ten years ago as we scratched out the concepts of school choice on a piece of paper." Those concepts had been tested in the Cleveland plan and challenged every step of the way by the education establishment, and here we were in the highest court in the land. All because one governor, George Voinovich, was willing to take a political risk to help kids in his home state; and another man, David Brennan, came along to help and never gave up.

"I understand the power of choice in the business world," Brennan told me more than once. "This is human nature and Economics 101. Nothing gets people's attention more than the loss of a few customers."

Brennan was not alone in this struggle to bring school choice to Ohio. There are other stalwarts: Judge Bill Batchhelder, Commissioner Mike Fox, Senator Pat Sweeney, Attorney General Betty Montgomery, and Governor Voinovich who created the commission that proposed the "voucher plan." And there are the school principals, the teachers, and especially the parents; those wonderful, faithful, persevering parents who kept this program alive in spite of everything the American Civil Liberties Union and the education establishment could throw at them.

But it was Brennan who brought the team together. He was the "go to" guy and everybody knew it. Together we met challenges from the American Federation of Teachers, the National Education Association, and the ACLU. We fought in the Franklin County Court, the state appellate Court, the Ohio Supreme Court, the Federal District Court, and the U.S. Sixth Circuit. Now we were here at last in the chambers of the United States Supreme Court. It felt good to finally be there. On February 20, 2002, the Ohio School Choice Plan was about to make history and Dave Brennan was there in the first row to see it all unfold.

It was back in 1993 when he phoned and asked me to stop by his Akron office. He is a very big man: six foot five, two hundred fifty something, and very hard to

3

miss in a crowd; especially when he wears his white Stetson, which is most of the time. We had worked briefly on a project or two before, but didn't know each other well. In his typically direct Brennan fashion he opened with, "The reason for this meeting is simple. I have just chaired a commission for Governor Voinovich on education reform. I met with the Governor and he told me your organization just blew up the outcome-based education plan in the state budget. He told me if I wanted school choice to work, I had better sit down and find out what you think about the idea. If you're against it, the Governor would like to know and save us both a lot of trouble."

I don't pretend to have that much power or savvy, but the respect was appreciated. We had just blown up another "top-down, flavor of the month" bureaucratic education plan, but that didn't mean we were against reform. Quite the contrary. We were looking for education alternatives that made sense and would place children first in the design, instead of at the end of the train.

It didn't take long to see Dave Brennan was on the same page. He had thought through the big philosophical, constitutional, and human nature issues of educational reform. He wasn't proffering a private agenda for his own purposes or gain. This was no Republican strategic plan to gain more political power.

(I'm a registered Independent.) He definitely wasn't trying to curry the favor of third-generation Ohio Republican bluebloods, who weren't exactly thrilled by his ideas.

This was a man committed to doing the right thing. He believed public education was leaving children behind, especially in the inner cities, and he viewed himself as part of the public that was supposed to do something about it. "Nobody," he told me, "should be denied the opportunity to learn to his maximum potential." (He had reached the point in life where the cause had crested over into his soul.)

How had this entrepreneur of medium (not immense) wealth reached this place in life? By now most people at his income level were building their third resort home and juggling vacation schedules nine months out of the year. Why was this man willing to ride to the front of the battle of education reform? In this book, he will tell you why and detail how. I know it began with his father.

Daniel Brennan was an old-fashioned GP, a family doctor, an Irishman from Boston who, David will tell you proudly, was the first Catholic to play football for Harvard. He went on to graduate from Harvard Medical School. He spoke Italian, Spanish, and German. At the start of World War I, he moved to

Akron where he found plenty of immigrants working in the tire industry who appreciated a doctor who shared their native language.

Dr. Daniel Brennan took care of anyone who needed his help. If his patients couldn't pay in cash, then apples or chickens would do. Growing up in the Depression '30s, war-torn '40s, and recovery '50s, young David learned from his father's example. Sure his dad was a doctor and a very important man in the community. That meant he had a greater burden to give; a greater responsibility to treat everyone with dignity.

Years later, the son would rise as a star in the world of accounting, then law, then manufacturing. In the tough world of the steel business, David would draw upon the lessons his dad had taught him. Everyone deserves respect. Everyone can learn. Everyone has a great gift of God-given potential.

David Brennan is a problem solver. He believes people can and do change for the better. In his manufacturing plants, he discovered his employees were hampered by poor basic learning skills. Many were functionally illiterate. Others were stymied by basic math. Not only had public education failed them, but this deficit was infecting whole families and communities. David and his partners decided to solve the problem by re-educating both employees and their families—

free of charge, as a free benefit. Employees, their children and, in some cases, their parents all went back to school—at work. What he learned in this process became a platform to address the bigger issue of educational reform.

In 1991, Pat Rooney pioneered the first major private scholarship programs for children in America's inner cities. Pat's efforts were followed by Ted Forstmann and John Walton with the Children's Scholarship Fund. While these leaders were working to bring private scholarships across the nation, Dave Brennan started looking to change educational opportunities for children in his home state of Ohio. The great news was that in 1990, Ohio voters had elected a new Governor who was looking for an opportunity to do exactly the same thing.

I first met George Voinovich in the mid '80s when he was mayor of Cleveland. He described himself then as "a kid from the neighborhood" trying to do the right thing for his city. Everyone agrees he did a great job for Cleveland; but the one thing that he couldn't fix, and that drove him crazy, was the poor condition of the Cleveland public schools. No matter how hard he tried, the inertia in the system and the bureaucratic resistance to change were massive barriers.

On election night 1990, I was with the Governor-elect for a few moments of reflection before he went out to do his victory speech. We spoke of trying to finish the work he began in Cleveland, of taking this next opportunity and making a difference in the lives of children and families. Just a few months into his new administration, the Governor called on me to help him assemble a task force on reforming and improving adoption and foster care laws and practices for families in Ohio. He called on Dave Brennan to chair another task force—the Governor's Commission on Educational Choice.

The Commission's final report was titled "The Ohio Scholarship Plan" and contained a proposal for two different plans. One permitted public school students K-12 to transfer to private schools with a scholarship if they lived in any of the 12 largest school districts in the state. The second plan limited participants to those entering the first grade, adding one additional grade per year. Both plans acknowledged the pivotal importance of permitting parents to choose the best school for their children.

Neither plan was ultimately adopted by the Ohio Legislature, but the ideas stimulated debate in the General Assembly and encouraged lawmakers to step into the waters of school choice. The outflow was the Cleveland Scholarship and Tutoring Plan, passed in

1995. This pilot program was the first in the nation to permit parents to choose the best public, private, or parochial school and pay any required tuition with a tax-funded scholarship. It also gave an equal number of tutoring scholarships to students who chose to remain in the public schools but who requested additional help.

The Governor's charge to the Commission was a statewide program. So why simply a pilot plan for children and parents in Cleveland? Governor Voinovich will tell you, "Because we have to crawl before we can walk and walk before we can run." Dave Brennan will tell you, "At the time, the lawmakers had such little hope that anything could fix the Cleveland schools, they were willing to take the risk. It was the best offer available that could get enough votes to pass." Even legislators carrying the endorsement of the teachers' unions figured things couldn't get worse in Cleveland. And they secretly hoped the voucher pilot would fail there and never return from exile.

Dave Brennan went to public grade school and Catholic high school. He has successfully accomplished three career paths: first as an accountant, then an attorney, and finally buying and building manufacturing companies. He is great with numbers and brilliant when it comes to writing and amending legislation. As Commission Chair, he utilized all his skill to create a balanced, reasonable and, most importantly, constitutional approach to school choice. As a lawyer he knew, we all knew, this case would be legally challenged with all the ferocity the educational establishment could muster. Together, David's team in and outside the Commission spent countless hours haggling over words and nuances that someday might be debated before the highest court in the land.

It was near agony getting the drafted legislation approved, but that was barely the beginning. Now the plan turned from the state capitol in Columbus to the streets of Cleveland. The Scholarship Plan was designed to serve families at or near federal poverty guidelines. The total maximum scholarship grant was $2,250. Parents, regardless of their poverty, were still required to pay 10 percent of the tuition themselves. Many schools were willing to accept this payment in hours served at the school in the lunch room or office, or in helping paint the building.

More than 30,000 Cleveland children came from families that economically qualified for this program. The state law made only 2,000 scholarships available. More than 7,000 scholarship applications were filed— so many that a lottery had to be held to award the scholarships. Obviously, word got out in Cleveland that hope was on the horizon.

Just as quickly, the teachers' unions slapped down their first lawsuits challenging the plan. Injunction after injunction in local and appellate courts delayed the full authorization of the program until August 12, 1996—a few weeks before schools were to open. The legal delays prevented non-public schools in Cleveland from expanding classroom capacity to accommodate new students. More than 350 parents had tuition scholarships but no classroom seats for their children.

Brennan, the problem solver, stepped in again. With only two weeks' lead time, he secured two school sites, hired a full staff and principal, and opened two brand new non-sectarian elementary schools grades K-3. His students came from the poorest households in Cleveland with an average taxable family income of less than $7,000. There was no way to tell that when you looked into their smiling faces and wonder-filled eyes. Brennan, and the amazing staff he assembled, never saw poor kids. They saw kids who could learn and accomplish great things. The Hope Academies were the only schools in the program, perhaps in the nation, composed totally of "voucher kids."

People came together from across the region with supplies, food for the cafeterias and books for the libraries. Parents volunteered to clean and paint classrooms. Teachers, business people and lawyers left their jobs drawn by the vision of the Hope schools. I'll never forget the first open house where the kindergartners sang their ABC's and read stories to their parents and community leaders. As the story of Hope unfolded, the Ohio House Education Committee and United States Congress held education committee hearings at the Hope Academies.

So why was each voucher worth only $2,250? In part, because some of the original drafters of the law, including Brennan, wanted to keep them that low. Their goal was to set a standard and try to maximize it. Brennan felt the obligation to show that, even if the number was too low, when using public money it was better to err on the low side than take advantage of taxpayers' support.

Ironically, in 2001, the Sixth Circuit Appellate Court would seize upon this well-intentioned standard and twist it to declare the program unconstitutional. The Court found the vouchers too low to attract participation from public schools in neighboring wealthier districts. In spite of all the legal effort to construct a truly neutral plan, a three judge panel in a 2-1 decision bought the ACLU's arguments. But in oral arguments on February 20, 2002, the U.S. Supreme Court did not appear to buy that same logic. The Supreme Court rightly questioned if a higher voucher alone would have persuaded affluent suburban public schools to accept vouchers and the kids from Cleveland? Does ice melt in a snowstorm?

So what has happened since vouchers came to Cleveland in 1996? Did all those terrible things predicted by voucher opponents befall the public school system? No, the Cleveland schools did not suffer an economic collapse. No, the voucher schools didn't capture all the best and brightest kids. No, vouchers didn't keep the Indians from winning the World Series. Today, in Cleveland, it is now OK to talk about real change. There are now charter schools in Cleveland, which the NEA helped launch nationally back in 1995, which it now regrets. Two school levies have also passed in Cleveland where none had passed in over 20 years. The district is conducting a $1.2 billion building renovation project, hiring more teachers, and test scores are up. And opponents said vouchers would ruin the public schools!

Never one to be afraid to look beyond a good idea, David Brennan got involved in the charter school movement, as well. His education management company, appropriately named White Hat Management, now manages 16 charter schools in Ohio, including six in Cleveland. He has pioneered a computer-based program to rescue high school dropouts. At risk-students who need to work as well as go to school can now attend a "Lifeskills Center" and earn a fully-certified high school diploma. They attend school in four-hour blocks each day, year round, and move forward on a personalized pace while holding down a job. Already, this new kind of high school has produced over 1000 high school graduates in Ohio. And David Brennan attends those graduation ceremonies every year.

School choice is based upon the principle that parents will, by and large, do what's best for their children. We all believe that to be true, but too often we let the headlines and prime-time television convince us parents don't care anymore. Back in 1999, we found out just how much parents care when Federal Judge Solomon Oliver tried to shut down the Cleveland scholarship program the day before school was to start. His decision threw almost 4,000 kids out of school.

As the *Baltimore Sun* reported (August 26, 1999), "The school year opened in a state of confusion yesterday, a day after a federal judge blocked a voucher program that lets Cleveland students attend private or religious schools...Nervous parents tied up phone lines as private school officials said they'd continue to accept vouchers pending an appeal."

Parents in the program didn't budge. The school choice leadership came together and refused to buckle under the intense pressure from the courts, the unions, and the school district.

The newspapers around the state and the nation assailed the judge's decision and, in just a few days, the judge attempted a compromise permitting existing students to stay in the program but rejecting 817 new students.

I remember calling David from the courthouse and telling him the decision. He asked what our School Choice Committee was going to do. I told him we would fight until every last one of those kids was back in class. And so our committee, led by The Ohio Roundtable, began to raise private funds to keep those kids in school; and the parents kept sending their kids to school in faith that somehow justice would prevail.

David got on the telephone and received pledges of financial support from national school choice leaders to provide sufficient funds to do just that, if necessary.

Ohio Attorney General Betty Montgomery stepped in and appealed the judge's order. The Sixth Circuit in Cincinnati sat on the appeal for weeks, forcing the appeal to the United States Supreme Court. Principals received no funds from the state, but refused to send a single voucher student home. Schools struggled to make payrolls and keep teachers from quitting. Then suddenly word came down from Washington D.C. that the U.S. Supreme Court had intervened, permitting the children to go back to school and stay there until the final appeals were ended.

And now we were sitting in the courtroom of that very same U.S. Supreme Court—David Brennan, Ann Brennan, and I—listening for the final time to the arguments we have carried in our hearts and minds since those early days in 1992. Except now those words are forever attached to the faces of children in Cleveland whose lives have been forever touched and changed.

If the Supreme Court rules in favor of school choice this June, every legislature in the nation will, at last, be free to begin a debate that is long overdue—a debate on the rights of parents to choose the best schools for their children. In the end, the real winners of this debate will be the children and their families. The heroes of this story will include George Voinovich, the tough kid from the neighborhoods of Cleveland who wanted to do the right thing; Betty Montgomery, the Attorney General who fearlessly did her job; and a tall man from Akron who wears a white cowboy hat and gets choked up when he sees children learning how to read.

David Brennan took on this challenge because he believed change was needed. Largely at his own expense, he launched a project that would alter thousands of lives, and, ultimately, write a page in American history.

Nature's law of inertia, that a body in motion tends to stay in motion, applies to human institutions as well. David did more than get the reform ball rolling. He has stayed in the battle to the end. People in power know most reformers run out of steam and fade away: This reformer did not.

Do I like the cowboy hat? After all these years, I still haven't decided. But the bottom line is this: When the key moment of opportunity came for somebody to stand up for parents and their children, David Brennan is the one who threw his hat in the ring. I thank God he did.

David Zanotti
The Ohio Roundtable and The School Choice Committee

1. An Idea on Trial

Inside and out, the United States Supreme Court may be the most impressive office structure in all Washington. My wife, Ann, thinks so, and she did her undergraduate work at Washington's Catholic University before she married me, had our children, went back to school and became a lawyer.

We are both lawyers, but it has been a while since either of us practiced. This winter, both of us intended to do our paperwork to be admitted before the bar of the United States Supreme Court. I've been authorized to practice before the District Courts and the Sixth Circuit Court of Appeals, and in each of those instances I was a party to the case. Being sworn in is a perfunctory procedure, but it is an honor and it is a special honor to say you've been admitted to practice before the Supreme Court.

But major surgery got in my way this time and, of course, in Ann's way, too. When, on February 20th we were not presented, I rationalized it as just as well. The doctors at Akron City Hospital did a great job, I was feeling better than ever, and I have plenty of plaques on the wall. We were there to hear oral arguments on *Zelman v. Simmons-Harris, No. 00-1751.* At issue was the constitutionality of the Cleveland tuition voucher program, and I know as much about the Cleveland tuition voucher program as anyone in the world. I chaired the Governor's Commission that developed the plan that generated the program that the teachers' unions have been fighting since before Day One.

The day before the hearing, the *New York Times* called this Supreme Court case "one of the most important church-state cases in the last decade." The *Hartford Courant* called it the "most closely watched case of the current session." And the *Financial Times* of London called it "the most important social policy issue of (the) current term." I was and am humbled by seeing the program I helped design and fought to maintain for a decade become the constitutional test of school vouchers open to private, sectarian, and public schools.

Bill Batchelder told me about the call he got one summer evening in 1995. He was in his office. It was after five and his secretary was gone. Ohio Governor George Voinovich—who has since become U.S. Senator George Voinovich—was on the line. I don't always agree with George on some of his positions in politics, but I'm not worried about that. It's enough that we have a person in office dealing honestly with issues and doing what he or she thinks is the right thing. And George always does. George has more integrity than any politician I have ever known. In this case, he and I were in complete agreement.

George was born and raised in Cleveland. He went to public and parochial schools and graduated from Collinwood High in 1954. Twenty-five years later, he was elected Cleveland's mayor. He was elected after the city defaulted on a $110 million debt in the administration of Dennis Kucinich, a Democrat—who redeemed himself later and is now in the U.S. Congress. But this was the first major default in the country since the Great Depression. George was so popular that in 1989 he was still mayor.

He had persuaded voters to raise the city's income tax by half a percent and had retired the debt. He had gen-erated a downtown building boom that finally ended the story Cleveland most hated: the one about the Cuyahoga River, once so polluted it actually burned.

Then he ran for governor. He beat the Democrat, Tony Celebrezze, Jr. easily in 1990 and swamped Bob Burch in 1994. (Ed. Note. Source of most data, *The Ohio Politics Almanac*, 1996, by Michael Curtin.) When he called Bill Batchelder, Governor George Voinovich already was in his second term.

Bill served in the Ohio House from 1968 through the first week of 1999. He was Speaker Pro Tempore when the Governor called. The Democrats had controlled the House from 1973 to 1994 and the Senate from 1975 through 1985. But now the Republicans had the majority in both houses, plus the governor's mansion.

I had something to do with that, and will explain that later. Bill was responsible for a great deal of work of the committees, even the ones he wasn't on. And he was a master of the language of legislation.

The Governor told Bill he was concerned about the potential language of part of the House budget bill—which would then go to committee and, in some form, return to him for signature. Bill answered "I think we can have that done by noon tomorrow," and he remembers a long silence. "I don't think that the Governor was sure it would work that way," he told me later. The part of the budget bill whose language the Governor wanted to be sure about was a program to provide tuition scholarships to up to 2,000 disadvantaged Cleveland children in kindergarten through the third grade. It had evolved or rather, been a compromise, out of a task force I had chaired for the Governor.

The Ohio economy had rebounded after a four-year recession, and George's budget was going to feature a tax cut. The scholarship part was going to create the Cleveland Scholarship and Tutoring Program. It would cost $5.25 million initially and be paid for by the state's Disadvantaged Public Impact Aid program. It would be the first program in the country in which tuition vouchers would be good in private, sectarian and public schools.

While downtown Cleveland had a renaissance culturally and in athletics, what had happened to the Cleveland public school system was anything but that. Cleveland had the great retro ballpark, Jacobs Field, for the Indians, and Gund Arena for the Cavaliers, and a restored theatre district. Gentrification was taking place by the river in an old warehouse area called "The Flats" and the Rock and Roll Museum was on the drawing board.

But, if you drove through East Cleveland, you could still see the remains of Hough, the area burned down in 1966. The half of Cleveland that could afford to move had moved to the suburbs. Sixty percent of the families left in Cleveland proper lived below the poverty line and 60 percent of its high school students didn't graduate. Talk about polar opposites!

The Governor wanted to be sure that the language of the bill created no difficulties with the First Amendment Establishment Clause of the U.S. Constitution: "Congress shall make no law respecting an establishment of religion, or prohibiting the free exercise thereof." There were Lutheran, Jewish, Muslim, and Catholic schools in Cleveland, as well as other private schools. Students, whose families would have to be below the poverty line to qualify, could use their vouchers at any school that would accept them, private or sectarian in Cleveland proper and public schools in the adjacent suburbs. Any student attending a Cleveland public school also could receive a grant for private tutoring.

The Governor said later that he believed even then that the Cleveland Program "would be the most genuine school-choice program of any in the country."

2. The Birth of the Plan

What Bill did that day was examine the *Lemon* case and the GI Bill. It was not as if he and the Republican caucus had not gone over this before; and so had I, many times. *Lemon v. Kurtzman* had been heard before the Supreme Court in 1971. Its ruling states that in order to survive a Constitutional challenge on Establishment Clause grounds, a law must first reflect a secular purpose. Its primary effect must neither advance nor inhibit religion. And it must avoid excessive government entanglement with religion. (Source: *Gatton v. Goff*, Court of Common Pleas, Franklin County, Ohio, July 31, 1996).

There was no question in my mind, Bill's, or the governor's that this program met all the qualifications. The bill would have a secular purpose because the statute permitted participation by private schools, parochial schools and all public schools in adjacent school districts; plus there was that tutoring grant. Its primary effect was not to advance religion; it was to empower inner city families with a choice and give their children a chance to escape poverty through a good education. And there was no government entanglement with religion; the vouchers would be the property of the parents and guardians who could use them in any school that would accept the children.

In drafting the legislation, much care was given to the issue that the parent's decision was the only reason these funds would end up at a particular school. For this reason, the payment from the Ohio Department of Education was made solely to the parent in the form of a draft that can ultimately be cashed only by a participating school. That is, the draft could not be used for any other purpose.

In contrast, the Milwaukee Voucher Plan—the first in the nation, which began in 1990—makes payment to the school and the parent jointly. Although this gives better control over the flow of the money, this also gives rise to the argument that the government is directing funds to a participating religious school. David Young, attorney for the Catholic Coalition in Ohio, and Ned Foley, an Ohio State University law professor, both emphasized the importance of this issue. In fact, David has always felt that this could be a crucial element in a final court decision as to the necessity for a "wholly independent action" sending the money to a religious school.

My organization established two schools for voucher students in 1996, known as HOPE Academies. In order to protect against unhappy parents refusing to endorse the checks over to the school, in our schools, at the point of application the parent was required to sign a Power of Attorney authorizing the school to: 1) direct the Ohio Department of Education to send the draft directly to the school; and 2) permit the school to endorse the draft over to the school.

As to the GI Bill, it had been approved by the federal courts. Some veterans had used the GI Bill to study at seminary. Roman Catholic seminaries. Fundamentalist Protestant seminaries. Yeshivas. Public universities. Private universities. Trade schools. Dance schools. It made no difference. "It seemed to me," Bill explained to me later, "that if we could get ourselves within those two cases, we would probably be all right. So that is what we did." And by noon the next day he, in fact, did have the language ready for the governor.

"It was a tough battle," he told a writer later, "but we finally got it passed as part of the budget bill," and that was one of the understatements of 1995.

Actually, the battle over choice had been going on at one level or another in Ohio since Mike Fox advanced vouchers in the House in 1976.

Mike Fox, of Hamilton, Ohio, was the first member of his family to go to college. At first he taught public school. In 1974 he ran for the state legislature, was elected at 25, and said to me later he was "ready to change the world." He served from 1975 to 1997. One of the changes he wanted to make immediately was to introduce a voucher option in the state.

"The people," he said, "ought to be able to send their children to the school of their choice." And did he try to make it happen. He tried to amend budgets, adding a voucher plan as a feature. Each budget cycle, he would come back with another amendment and every one would fail. He said later that, over time, he learned from the experience. And so did I.

George Voinovich once suggested that it was important for people like me not to oversell our programs. "Because when you do," he said, "the people who are your enemies want to get up and knock your hat off." And I have a very big hat. "It's important to engage," he said, "but the main thing is to stay alive so that you can demonstrate over a period of years that this thing works." I don't know that I was ever particularly low-key.

In spite of George's advice, we went ahead full bore. Mike Fox and I both stayed alive. Along the way, we realized that it would take the election of a Republican legislature to make something happen.

We knew we would continue butting our heads against that proverbial stone wall as long as the Ohio General Assembly was controlled by people elected by the strongest single lobby in the state: the Ohio Federation of Teachers and Ohio Education Association. It would be unfair to say that union teachers are only for union teachers and not for their students. But I would not go so far as to say the same about the union leadership.

Eventually, Mike concurred with the recommendations of the Governor's Task Force that I chaired—and that was either to pilot vouchers in 12 urban centers or pilot them statewide, but only one grade at a time. Mike had become majority chairman of the House education committee as a result of the election of 1994. Even so, the pilot(s) became "pilot," a far cry from Mike's dream; but it was just that, a pilot.

But at least we had gotten there. How could urban Democratic legislators vote against such a test when this inner-city system was in such bad shape?

Bill Batchelder gives much credit for the bill's passage to the Governor, to Mike Fox, to fellow Republican Jim Buchy and to Democrat representative Pat Sweeney, "who stuck his neck out and lost his (Democratic minority) leadership over the issue."

And he credits me, an Akron businessman who had been on an advisory committee to the public school board for three years and had quit in frustration. "Without David Brennan," he said, "it wouldn't have happened." I would like to think so.

"That the General Assembly intended the program to truly operate as a pilot project is demonstrated by Section 45.35 of Am. Sub. H.B. 117," wrote Judge (Franklin County Court of Common Pleas) Lisa L. Sadler, in her July, 1996, decision that first upheld the statute. The bill, she continued, "required the superintendent to contract with an independent researcher" to "evaluate the pilot project to determine the impact of such things as student attendance, performance on standardized test scores, parental involvement, and the economic impact on the school districts."

Mike Fox didn't get a reserved ticket to the Supreme Court hearing on February 20, so he was one of the people who slept outside the courthouse the night before in order to get in line. He deserved better, and I'm glad he got a seat.

3. The Commission

In listening to the arguments in the Supreme Court on February 20, 2002—a decade after the recommendations of the task force—it seemed to me that, in their questioning, the justices hit all the points we had considered when the legislation was established. As much as a plan could be designed to be constitutionally correct, I believed then and believe now, it was so designed. I am very proud that the commission's work helped bring the issue of school choice to the U.S. Supreme Court.

So how had school choice finally surfaced as a pilot program in Cleveland?

Looking back in 2000, Bill Batchelder said he was first spurred to action by "numerous industrialists, business people (and) bankers concerned they would have to leave Cleveland. They were saying they could not get employees within the city who had the ability to do the jobs they had available."

Cleveland had more than 900,000 people in the 1950 U.S. Census and little more than half that in the early 1990s. Many of the families who were sending their children to suburban schools did not want to go downtown every day. Batchelder told a writer that "They were afraid."

One of the bankers told him he never thought he would face a situation where he would even think of moving his bank from the city of Cleveland. "I felt," Batchelder said, "we had a moral obligation to try to see that young people who come from very limited backgrounds economically would have the opportunity to improve themselves."

George Voinovich looked back at when he was mayor. His own children were in the system. At first they had received an excellent education, and then, he said, "it deteriorated to the extent" a teacher advised him "they shouldn't go into the seventh grade because it was not what it should be." He found, he told a writer, "this vast number of youngsters not getting the kind of education they ought to be getting. What we need in this country to be successful," he said, is to search out options and "invest in them to see if there isn't a better way. How well we do that, in particular in our urban areas, is going to have a lot to say about the future of our country."

He and I had come to the same conclusion, and the Governor already was aware of my feelings. *Cleveland Plain Dealer* columnist Dick Feagler wrote (December 11, 1996) that when he had attended the Cleveland public schools, he "didn't feel short-changed." But that over time, "society has gone to hell...and the Cleveland schools went with it." He had, he wrote, "heard 15 years' worth of school superintendents arrive in Cleveland to announce that a whole generation of children has been lost."

When the Governor created the commission to search out options to be tested within Ohio, he asked me to chair it. The Governor's Commission on Educational Choice was appointed in April 1992. It had 29 members (Appendix A), including leadership from businesses and corporations, two classroom teachers, a former head of the Ohio PTA, two school district superintendents and several school board members. Our charge from the Governor was to develop a plan to implement "choice" throughout Ohio. The commission recommended "that several pilots be initiated in specially designated areas as a prelude to state-wide implementation." What eventually passed in the legislature was the single pilot in Cleveland.

I was very pleased when Senator Voinovich acknowledged that I believed fervently that "the future of America is in our educational system"...that I had spent "my time and money and stress and strain to make it happen," and that I could have been "down in Florida playing golf every day...or investing in manufacturing widgets."

Instead, I chaired the task force that recommended field-testing vouchers, and, in 1996, I formed the first group to open new inner-city, non-sectarian schools once the Cleveland voucher legislation passed. But I must confess, I still play some golf and some of my companies continued to manufacture "widgets."

By 1996, a federal judge already had ordered the state to take control of the Cleveland district. "In the Cleveland district, half of the teachers are afraid of the kids," Mrs. Beverland Paul told *Education Week* (February 19, 1997), which was why she was now sending her children to a voucher school, where she liked the discipline and mandatory uniforms. Authority for the Cleveland School system was later turned over to the city's mayor—Michael R. White until 2001, and then, Jane Campbell.

Patrick Sweeney, then a ranking Democratic state representative who represented the west side of Cleveland, broke ranks to support vouchers, and he was one of the harshest critics of our opponents. As a result, he lost his minority party leadership post.

Sweeney looked to the Head Start Program as a model for the Cleveland voucher program when the legislation was being written. He had been in the Ohio General Assembly for 32 years and had been trying to aid non-public schools since 1967.

Head Start, he said, was universally accepted. It was funded at the state and the federal level. The programs, he said, "are being run in the black churches all across America and nobody is talking about Church-State relations there. We have choice grants, Pell grants and instructional grants, student loans going to kids that go to private colleges. And no problem."

He also was particularly critical of some of the national leaders of his party who, he said, "never send their children to public schools but come out foursquare against vouchers. People who have an opportunity to write a check," I remember him saying, "have a voucher in their pocket. What they don't want are children...who are in this neighborhood, and in this inner city...to have a checkbook." He advocated a 30-district voucher system for Cuyahoga County. I will always remember him saying that "if you don't have them by fourth grade, we have them in the prison system or in the welfare system."

The teachers unions' objections to vouchers, I also remember him saying, "had nothing to do with the First Amendment. It's all about protecting control of the funds going to K-12."

Vouchers in Ohio originally had *not* been a clear cut partisan issue. John Gilligan, a Democratic governor (1971-1975) had tried to get a $100 to $200 tuition tax credit. It was a Democratic measure and it passed. It was blocked by the Ohio Supreme Court, but the opposition was the American Civil Liberties Union, not the education establishment. Sweeney said later that "the education people didn't care because it wasn't big bucks and they saw it as just throwing a few bones to the Catholic school system."

In late 1995, a *Cleveland Plain Dealer* editorial (Nov. 26) put the Cleveland Tuition Voucher Program in perspective: "While populists and politicians prattle about the way to save the Cleveland school system, 1,500 (eventually 1,994) children could have a chance for a better education as soon as next year....True, the effort will serve about 2 percent of the system's 74,000-student enrollment, far shy of the statewide effort once envisioned...Even so, the very existence of an alternative for local children is a reason to rejoice."

To reach this point had taken the recommendations of the Governor's Task Force and a legislative process in which the recommendations of the Ohio Scholarship Plan were killed and reborn and killed again.

As only Pat Sweeney could explain it, he said, "First, it was going to be in eight or ten locations around the state. Then it was going to be universal. Finally, they kicked out a pilot plan for Cleveland. Normally, a pilot program is something you want to learn from. A leader of my own party sat up and said, 'We don't want to learn anything from this.' They don't want to learn. They know what the kids are going to get. They know the inner-city kids are going to jump at the opportunity to leave the public school network." And, in 1996, they did.

In spite of all the problems facing families in the inner cities—including that they pay 10 percent of the $2,500 tuition—there were more than 7,000 applications for the 1,994 scholarships eventually available for the 1996-1997 school year. Some 350 students ended up with scholarships but no class space.

That was when we opened our two non-sectarian schools. We called them HOPE Academies. The name was not copied from the Hope Scholarship Program in Arkansas. We actually came first. David Zanotti, president of the Ohio Roundtable, suggested it to me. At first HOPE was an acronym for "Help Our Private Education." One of our parents explained it to a reporter as "Help Our People's Education," and that's what it remained.

The schools were finally opened after a restraining order was sought to prevent the Cleveland program from getting under way, and was denied, unanimously, by the Franklin County Court of Appeals. The date was August 12, 1996.

Cleveland's two Hope Academies had less than three weeks to get everything and everyone ready for classes to begin. And that is what we did. Many people were responsible for making that happen: my daughter, Nancy Brennan; John Morris; Ann Yarman; Lori Wenger; and the entire staff of "A Better Way of Life," an Akron GED center we had been operating since 1990.

Because the idea required a very serious change in education policy, we encountered intense opposition. I am not bothered by the opposition you're required to deal with when you propose serious change. That's the stuff that fleshes out an idea. It sharpens your ideas and removes the rough edges. It brings you down to the essence of what you are trying to do. The core of what we are trying to do is close the achievement gap between children of poor families and the children of wealthier families.

Legislatures are the boiling pot of ideas. We all know that wonderful line: Never watch sausage or legislation being made. That's because legislation is messy. It is amazing to me that we come out with what we do. It's the give and take and the back and forth. Legislation should be evolutionary. I didn't believe that ten years ago. Now I've concluded all successful revolutions are evolutionary.

4. Black Robes, White Hats

Whether the Establishment Clause prohibits Ohio's program from authorizing parents to use scholarships at any private school of their choice, religious or otherwise.

In the U.S. Supreme Court, the justices enter the room through curtained porticos behind the dais. They come out at the same time and, as the Court Clerk does his "Oyez, Oyez," everyone stands until the justices are seated and the Clerk announces the Court is in session. On February 20, 2002, Justice Ruth Bader Ginsburg read a decision involving Medicaid funding, then 25 or so attorneys were admitted to the bar, the clerk administered the oath, and the proceedings began.

Meanwhile, outside, hundreds of demonstrators, for both sides, rallied on and around the courthouse steps. In November, we had gained support from a bipartisan group of nearly three dozen elected officials led by New York Mayor Rudolph Giuliani who, as the *Plain Dealer* reported (November 10, 2002) had found time to turn his attention to the issue "with the vigor he used to battle terrorism and root for the Yankees."

Among the other friends of the court who had filed briefs were former Baltimore Mayor Kurt Schmoke, and Milwaukee Mayor John Norquist, both Democrats; our own Councilwoman from Hough, Fannie Lewis; and the governors of three states and the attorneys general of seven. So did the Union of Orthodox Jewish Congregations of America; the U.S. Conference of Catholic Bishops; and the National Association of Independent Schools. A spokesman for Ohio Attorney General Betty Montgomery, Joe Case, said that our lawyers had never seen this kind of support in any other case.

Judith French, age 39, and recently promoted to chief counsel in the office of Betty Montgomery, had been in Washington for nine days preparing our case with her co-counsel. Although it was only her second argument before the Supreme Court, and though she had not argued the case earlier in the U.S. Court of Appeals, she had the complete confidence of those who knew her or her reputation. And that certainly included me. The Ohio Attorney General's Office had recently won a number of national awards for advocacy. Judi French was one of the main reasons for them. And, as the *Cleveland Plain Dealer* reported that day, she also was wearing her two good-luck bracelets.

Clint Bolick of the Institute of Justice had argued or briefed every major school-choice lawsuit in the country. He is highly respected for these efforts, and rightly so.

While Clint had made a major effort to have Betty Montgomery hire a more experienced attorney to argue the case, Betty had demurred, as she honestly felt Judi would do an excellent job.

Events showed Betty's judgment to be correct. In the words of Kenneth Starr, the former Whitewater independent counsel and Solicitor General of the United States, Judith French presented "one of the finest oral arguments I have ever witnessed."

Ken himself was in the "second chair." He had argued some 30 cases before this Court and, in 1998, had been successful before the Wisconsin Supreme Court on behalf of Wisconsin's voucher program, which is limited to Milwaukee. He had helped Judi prepare her legal briefs and had been prepping her all week. Joining them was Columbus attorney David J. Young, who would address the Court on behalf of the private petitioners.

They were joined by Theodore Olson, the current Solicitor General of the United States, arguing on behalf of President George W. Bush, who hoped to place a voucher program in his U.S. education bill. Olson had argued the case that settled the Presidential election, and had been before the high court some 15 times.

Arguing for the plaintiffs was Robert Chanin, 67, with a 33-year career as general counsel for the National Education Association and with four cases before the Supreme Court and briefs filed in nearly every Supreme Court case involving church-state issues since 1983. Joining him was New York attorney Marvin Frankel.

Just the day before, in Wisconsin, that state's Supreme Court had ruled 4-2 against a challenge to that state's voucher program, the one Ken Starr had defended successfully in 1998. Now, the Wisconsin court had found the challenge "frivolous," "filed in bad faith" and impugning the court's integrity (*Milwaukee Journal-Sentinel*, February 20). "School choice," concluded the *Journal-Sentinel* article, "lets low-income students attend private and religious schools with taxpayer-funded vouchers. The 1998 ruling said the program was not an unconstitutional endorsement of religion."

But what of Ohio?

"I can't recall a recent day at the court that had such a feeling of being a major watershed moment," a Clinton era acting Solicitor General, Walter Dellinger, told the *Washington Post*. In its coverage, the *Post* took pains to point out that the Ohio vouchers of $2,250 were "too low to pay for most independent private schools and no suburban public schools had taken the state's offer of aid in exchange for admitting inner-city children.... so most of the 4,300 Cleveland voucher students have ended up in church-run schools."

Had the voucher figure been larger, which many voucher supporters would have preferred, would the situation have been the same? "A central legal question," explained the *Post*, "...is whether the outcome reflects free choices by students and their families or the program offers no realistic alternative."

Are there realistic alternatives? In the courtroom, Ted Olson explained that about 16,000 Cleveland students now attend tuition-free magnet schools and 2,000 tuition-free community schools, all public "charter schools" each with its own school board. French then said the result is a "neutral program," neither favoring nor discriminating against public, private religious or private non-sectarian schools.

However, in the year 2000 decision that had struck down the Cleveland voucher program, a federal appeals court had declared the charter school alternative an entirely different program. "How is it," Justice Sandra Day O'Connor asked, "that we look only at the voucher program?" Olson told Judge O'Connor that, in his opinion, the appeals court had made "a legal error."

The *Boston Globe* pointed out the next day that, should the Supreme Court decide that in Cleveland "the role of the charter schools is critical, it could choose to send the case back to the appeals court."

In late February 2001, the Sixth Circuit Court of Appeals in Cincinnati had refused to reconsider a 2-1 ruling by a three-judge federal panel that had found the Cleveland program unconstitutional. By that time, though the highest court four times had refused to rule on other church-state disputes—in Arizona, Maine, Pennsylvania and New York—both sides of the Ohio case thought the appeals ruling would end up in Washington.

The Arizona case had challenged a $500 state tax credit for donating money for private-school grants and scholarships. In Maine, vouchers were subsidizing students who attend some private schools but not religious schools. In Pennsylvania, religious publications were not being exempted from state sales taxes. In New York, Hassidic Jews were attempting to revive a public school district that served disabled children in their community. In December, the Court refused to disturb a Vermont Supreme Court ruling denying tuition aid to students in parochial schools.

However, on November 5, 1999, the highest court in the land, in a 5-4 decision, had lifted U.S. District Court Judge Solomon Oliver Jr.'s injunction that had blocked new students from enrolling in the Cleveland Voucher Program. Some people considered it an extraordinary action, as the Court, they said, rarely overturns a lower-court injunction. While this was "a great victory for Ohio's voucher program," Betty Montgomery said then that she recognized it was not the end of the case. By this time, Robert A. Taft II, also a school-choice advocate, had followed George Voinovich as Governor of Ohio.

The four justices who had voted to retain the injunction were John Paul Stevens, David H. Souter, Ruth Bader Ginsburg and Stephen G. Breyer. Those in the majority were Chief Justice William H. Rehnquist, Anthony M. Kennedy, Clarence Thomas, Antonin Scalia and Sandra Day O'Connor. They are the same nine justices who made the decision on the merits of *Zelman v. Simmons-Harris.*

Justice O'Connor had been seen as the deciding vote in the 1999 case that had lifted the injunction. Little appeared different to me on February 20, 2002. If there were to be a 5-4 vote, prognosticators expected her to swing the decision. "She gave little away," as Linda Greenhouse wrote in the *New York Times* the next day. Justice O'Connor, Greenhouse continued, was "pressing both sides and expressing some skepticism about the answers she received."

It was Justice O'Connor who suggested that our program might be viewed as just one part of a larger school reform effort, including the charter schools. But it was she who also asked Judi French whether ruling in favor of *Zelman* would require overruling the *Nyquist* decision. What was *Nyquist?* In 1973, the Court ruled in *Nyquist* that a New York tuition assistance program only for students in private schools, most of the schools being sectarian, was unconstitutional.

No, Judi answered, it would not require overruling *Nyquist*. The Ohio program gives parents an option, including receiving extra money for tutoring or transferring to other public schools. When Judge Souter said that, nevertheless, the Ohio and New York programs appeared to have the same effect, Judi responded that in Ohio the money flowed not because of government action, but because "that's what the parents have chosen."

A majority of the Court has repeatedly held that a plan which is neutral on the face, subject only to the wholly independent choice of the consumer, is constitutional.

The minority of the court would decide constitutionality on the effect of the plan. In other words, if 99 percent of the students are actually in religious schools, thus the plan is unconstitutional. As one of the justices queried, "Must we determine each year whether the plan is constitutional or unconstitutional based on actual school enrollments?" Such a measure creates great uncertainty, and the Court has decided that such a test is not appropriate.

Then Justice Breyer said that, though he did not want them exposed to religious messages, for the sake of their education, he would send his own children to parochial schools if he were living in Cleveland (*New York Times*, February 21).

That day, the argument continued for 80 minutes, 20 beyond the high court norm. "Ohio," Chanin argued, "has the right to make an unsound educational judgment, but not an unconstitutional one." I believe we made neither.

When Justice O'Connor asked Solicitor General Olson whether the Cleveland program made any "effort to make sure that the money which ends up in the parochial schools is not used for religious training," he had to reply that it did not. But, he said, attending sectarian schools was a "genuinely independent private choice," and he asked the justices to bear in mind that the "history, context and purpose" of the program was to rescue Cleveland children from "a manifestly failing system."

"Critics who fear the ramifications of a ruling in favor of the program compare the scope of the case to *Brown v. Board of Education*—the landmark 1954 school desegregation lawsuit," The *Hartford Courant* had written a day earlier. "If the court clears the way for the Cleveland program to continue, they say, it's just a matter of time before cities around America will follow suit and public school coffers drain into religious schools."

I have always disagreed. It's just a matter of time, I believe, before competition will force the public schools to do a better job, thus raising the quality of primary and secondary education for students all across America and, in particular, in its inner cities.

That has been my personal goal since I entered this fray. I thrived on competition on the way to becoming successful as an accountant, an attorney, a manufacturer, and now some call me "an educator." I am proud of that appellation and prouder yet of just having completed a nine-year term on the Board of Trustees of my undergraduate alma mater, a public university, The Ohio State University. Along the way, I have come to respect the dignity of every human being and to know that "every child can learn." Here is why, and how, it all started.

5. Why it All Started

I often say everything I have done right in my life I did for the wrong reasons. But that's OK, because I have instinctively understood that something better was going to turn up. I did not go into manufacturing because I wanted to be a humanitarian and did not get involved in education because I wanted to be an activist. But here I am.

"Everybody in the world wants the 'three P's': Peace in the world. Peace in their lives. And a Piece of the action." I first heard that from a motivational psychologist at Worthington Industries. John McConnell built Worthington Industries from the ground up and made it one of America's great companies by making it one of America's great places to work.

I visited John when my partners, Dick Hamlin and Jim McCready, and I were buying manufacturing plants, and I learned more than a few things from him. It was the summer of 1982. People don't remember that until about 1985, the American way in a factory was "my way or the highway." When the red light comes on, you turn the lever to the right, and if you ask why you can't turn it left, you're fired.

John was the first person to quote Napoleon to me when he said, "Give me enough medals to award the troops and I'll conquer the world." John had one of the finest employee involvement programs in the country. He already knew that an army fights on its stomach: He had instituted an excellent profit-sharing program for his employees. Napoleon must have run out of medals at Waterloo. John never has.

My partners and I once owned numerous manufacturing plants. In Ohio. In Michigan. In South Carolina and North Carolina. In Texas. In Alabama. All over. They made steel and wheels and stamped parts and things like that. In our typical company, more than 20 percent of pretax profits went in cash to our employees every three months. They were so involved in making more money, we made more. It never cost us a dime.

We also hired John McConnell's company to do training for our people for three years, and then we developed our own staff.

We would take everyone away to a retreat within the first few months. Everybody. We would break up into groups of 18, each with two facilitators. Friday night was graduation. I went to every graduation for ten years. I'd have men and women stand up and talk about themselves and their experiences. They didn't have to, but about two-thirds always wanted to. And you know who benefited most? I did.

In a business context, money is how you keep score. But I used to give talks to my employees and explain that we were not in business to make a profit. Neither were we in business to make a loss. We were in business to satisfy our customers. If we did that, we would make that profit. If we did that, our customers would stay our customers. I carry that philosophy to school choice; providing there is a choice. The only accountability you need for choice is consumer demand, and the possibility of job loss if that demand is not satisfied.

The beginning? The beginning of my passion for educational choice was when I realized in the late 1980s that my efforts to convince the Akron public schools that what we were doing so successfully to educate people in my companies was being ignored by them. There was really no way to influence anybody to even *try* what we were doing.

It was quite frustrating, and I really can empathize with every parent who has to have felt that way when something didn't go right. I could not get a credible response from anyone. No one was responsible for making a decision. I was fighting a big marshmallow. Push on it and nothing happens.

For three or four years, working in the Akron Public Schools, I had been very active. I went to an advisory committee meeting one night, and the agenda was the same as the one three years before, and that was it; that and a little fable my wife, Ann, brought back at about the same time from a meeting of the Heritage Foundation. It went like this:

> *Envision a law that required you to buy a Buick every three years. And, whether you wanted one or not, you had to pay a Buick tax even if you declined to take the car. That didn't prevent you from buying a Chevrolet or a Plymouth (if these alternatives existed), but you still had to pay the Buick Tax.*
>
> *What would happen to the quality of Buicks under this scenario? What would happen to the cost of Buicks with this lock on the market?*

Of course, two predictable things would happen. The cost of Buicks would keep going up. The quality of Buicks would keep going down.

That simple analogy, combined with my experience with the public schools' bureaucracy, began my conversion.

The solution to a monopoly, of course, is competition. We citizens want the right to buy whatever car we please. Given that, to compete in the marketplace, various manufacturers would have to produce high quality products or we wouldn't buy them. And, as much as possible, costs would be driven down as the many companies strived to stay competitive.

I began to read whatever I could find on school choice. I discovered that the economist and Nobel Prize winner Milton Friedman had espoused school choice as far back as 1955.

I found *Market Education* by Andrew Colson, a disciple of Friedman, in which he recites how the argument of government versus private education can be traced far back in recorded history.

One of his early examples is Athens and Sparta: Sparta, the demanding socialist state, with rigid government control of education; Athens, the cradle of democracy, with unlimited opportunities to educate. The cultural and democratic history of the Western world stands on the shoulders of Athens, while there is not one thing we carry on from Sparta. When people are allowed to create and innovate, they do.

So, we are a threat and they are a monopoly. They may soon have to make better Buicks.

6. How it All Started

Fred Schoen was the CEO at our Spartanburg, South Carolina plant. Two employees there were Anna Mathews and Jay Guess. Both would probably have been replaced when we automated the plant because of their lack of basic reading and math skills. But by then we had developed our company learning centers. Anna ended up running the Spartanburg learning center and Jay became a foreman. Another employee, who lived in an adjacent town, excitedly came up to Fred one day.

"There's a sign right outside my town," he said. "I've lived there 40 years and I never knew what that sign said. That's the name of my town on that sign."

Once, when I was visiting the plant, an employee came into Fred's office because he knew I was there. He proudly pulled a card from his pocket and showed it to me. It was his library card.

We had bought our first company in 1975. For the first seven or eight years, we didn't do anything different from anyone else. In 1982, I went to a brake plant in Berea, Kentucky. We were thinking about buying it, but we didn't. Berea is famous as the home of Berea College, which provides full scholarships for its 1500 students from Appalachia. As a result, this remote section of southern Kentucky has a highly educated work force.

Shortly after I walked into the plant, the manager asked me if I wanted to go down to the factory floor. When we got there, he introduced me to the foreman, excused himself and left.

The foreman and I talked for a few minutes, and then the foreman took me over to the first machine and introduced me to the operator. As I was talking to the operator, the foreman walked away.

The operator had me sit in the seat and showed me how to operate the controls of the machine. A few minutes later, he took me over to another machine, and he introduced me to that operator and left.

This went on for a couple of hours during which time I did not see any management. I simply talked to the workers, one on one. I was stunned. The pride the workers had in their environment, as well as in their work, was so strong I could feel it. Each work area was spotless. Each operator had his (or her) nameplate on his machine. The plant had profit-sharing as well as exceptional morale.

Soon, we negotiated to buy a plastics factory in Michigan. We were to go up to the plant and close the deal the next day. I told Ann, "I'm going to do what they do in Berea. I'm going on the factory floor and personally introduce myself to every single employee."

That night I didn't sleep. I was scared to death. I had no idea what reaction I would get. I tossed and turned all night. But I had made up my mind. When I got to the plant and told the manager what I was doing, he thought I was bonkers. However, we went down to the factory floor, and a wonderful thing happened.

The employees were warm and enthusiastic about meeting me. Nancy Bishop introduced herself to me as Chairman of the Plant. I didn't understand at the time that that was her title in the union. I had not known that the union had the same officer designations as the company.

In 1986, we bought a steel mill. By then, it was routine for me to walk all over the plant introducing myself. It was stunning. The people would tell me they had never met an officer of the parent company, much less the Chairman of the Board. Some had worked there 30 years.

I had grown up in the years of the Depression and World War II. Corporate America was extremely authoritarian then. We had emerged from the war as the strongest economic power in the world and a top-down, command and control, hierarchical, industrial society. Like most manufacturing executives, I had come to consider labor as just another factor in production. Individuals were just another resource. Not only that, I assumed that all workers wanted was a paycheck and, for that, they would grudgingly give a certain amount of work. Just as it had been in the military, personal aspirations were not a corporate concern.

I had not always been a manufacturing CEO, by any means. After college, I started as a work-a-day accountant with a 40-hour job, had quit to build my own bookkeeping business, then became a lawyer and struggled to build that business.

Once, Ann and I had had to sell some furniture to make ends meet. I invested in a frozen custard stand and lost all my money. I invested in furniture manufacturing, and lost it again; and in a hotel chain, and lost it a third time. I continued to be a young man in a hurry, and somewhere along the way lost a lesson of childhood along with my investments.

My physician father had been adamant that every single person has value and every single person deserves respect. As a child and as a young man, I had witnessed bravery, pride, and dignity in his working class patients. Of all the things I have learned in life, this was the most important.

Through the experience of Berea and ones in my own plants that followed, I began to look beyond the impersonal "work force" to the personal "worker," beyond the forest to the trees. More and more, the workers were black, Hispanic, or Asian, from different cultures and many different countries. They were people I would not have known otherwise. I began to truly appreciate how we all want the same things out of life. In time, I would empathize with them and change how we dealt with all our employees.

Some of my friends note today that I'm sometimes the only one to thank the waitress or the first to thank the car valet. Perhaps I am. I know that for many years now I have thanked our factory workers personally for what they do and the pride they have in their work. Everyone goes through a continuous growth in life. I am glad I relearned such an important lesson about the common bond of humanity while I was still in a position to do something about it.

My reawakening in our factories grew into a concept of social justice that, in some ways, led to the Cleveland Scholarship and Tutoring Program.

While the Buick analogy, and my reading Colson, Friedman, and others fostered my conversion to school choice, what clinched my decision to act upon it was a visit in 1990 to St. Adalbert School in inner-city Cleveland. This was a Catholic parish school of some 400 students. All the students were minorities, all from the inner-city poor. The principal was Lydia Harris.

The comportment and accomplishments of her students were incredible. All of her students go on to high school and graduate. Ninety percent go on to college. That had been going on for many years and continues to this day. When I asked Lydia if the program could be replicated, her reply was that we could do it endlessly. Armed with that knowledge, pushing for vouchers for more children made enormous sense to me, and strongly motivated me to let that happen.

After Lydia retired from St. Adalbert in 1998, she worked as a consultant for White Hat Management and, for three years, has been principal of Hope Academy, Broadway Campus. She is an inspiration.

7. Corporate Learning Centers

In the United States of America, if we business people have too many employees, we can lay them off. No other industrial society permits this to the same extent. Not Canada. Not Japan. Not England. Not anywhere else in the Common Market. I have come to believe that this enormous right gives us, as employers, two moral obligations to our employees.

The first is to be forthright and explain that, "We cannot guarantee you a job for a month, a year, or a lifetime. That depends on the good will of our customers. Should they stop using our products or services, no matter how good our intentions, you may lose your job."

The second is to explain that, "While you are with us, we have an obligation to you to maximize your education and training. If termination ever comes, you will have maximum reemployment potential. When new opportunities arise here, you will be competent to compete." The parallel easily can be made to my attitude about the business of education.

In 1987, in our Spartanburg plant, we opened our first of what we call "learning centers." Some of our employees did not know how to read. Some would even tell us they believed we faked it when we read. Many would not believe, or allow us to know they believed, that a better education could better their lives.

In 1987, the average reading and mathematical skills of the 600 employees in Spartanburg tested at the fifth grade. But by 1995, they tested at the 10th grade!

George Cherpas, our Human Resources Vice President, had stumbled across a small center in an industrial park doing literacy work on a contract basis. They were using something new called "computerized instruction." Their software package was a primitive black and white program called "Wicat." I investigated Wicat and became convinced we should try it. We already had brought school teachers to the plant to give classroom instruction. It was a failure. We had learned that our employees who had not done well in a classroom as children did not do well in a classroom as adults. Expecting a different result, we discovered, was ridiculous, if not insane.

We also discovered, to no one's surprise, that those who most needed the education were last to volunteer for it. Traditional public education had convinced them they were dumb. "I come to work every day on time," they would protest. "Why do you insist on humiliating me?" We therefore made education mandatory and paid our employees for it: One or two hours a week, depending upon their level of need to develop basic educational skills.

After a year or so working two hours a week with the computer self-learning program, the reluctant students forgot they were "dumb." They knew they weren't. They realized they could learn anything. Wow!

Soon we discovered that our employees' educations were causing family fights and jealousies. Some mates were envious. Some just hoped for the same educational opportunities. We gave them *all* the opportunity. We extended the program to the families, including the children, and discovered that each helped the other advance. We not only were educating our employees, we were helping solidify family bonds.

When we installed sophisticated computerized machinery in that plant, because we had upgraded their reading and math skills, we were able to develop the operators and technical people from within. Otherwise, they would have lost their jobs. Spartanburg became a world-class stamping plant, doing world-class work because of the educational investment we made in our employees.

In the early 1990s in North Carolina, BMW put its first North American assembly plant less than five miles from one of our steel products companies.

BMW paid $17 an hour for the same type of work while our people earned $10 an hour. All the workers in our factory were using the learning center, as were their spouses and children. We did not lose one employee to BMW.

By that time, we also had established an "A Better Way of Life" Learning Center in downtown Akron to teach basic skills to welfare recipients. Job training is little help to a person who cannot read, or do basic math. Using referrals from the government, this center became the most successful welfare education program in the county. The adults who participated were not stigmatized by having to go to school. Instead, they participated in computer training. As a result, the dropout rate was considerably less than the 90 percent experienced by most adult education remedial courses. Successful students would obtain their GED.

The average middle-class student comes to kindergarten with a 3,000 to 4,000 word vocabulary. The average inner-city student comes with 500 words. It's not rocket science to give that child 2,500 more words. You shouldn't have to be sledge-hammered to buy into that one. There are computer programs that do that beautifully. When any of us reads new material, if five percent of the text consists of unknown words, through context we can figure most of them out and add to our vocabulary. If 20 percent or more is unknown—we're dead.

The computer can give an underachiever an incredibly intensive injection of information which, by and large, is very pleasing because a successful accomplishment rate is in that student's own control. For the first time in their lives, just like our adults in our plant learning centers, these students become really convinced "I am not dumb." Every other experience in school may have convinced them otherwise. Computer instruction can be a magical breakthrough for the underachiever.

In 1990, our company donated $150,000 each to two schools in Akron for computer laboratories like the ones in our learning centers. You just don't install computers. You install a teaching system based upon individual instruction. Without technology, neither schools nor industry can ever provide that. Simply putting technology in the classroom is the wrong approach. It's like buying a youngster a car before he knows how to drive.

One school was Akron St. Vincent grade school, with about 300 students. The other was Robinson public grade school, with about 700 children in the heart of the poorest section in town. Joanne Loveless, the teacher at St. Vincent told me that, in a 45-minute session, many mathematics students could do 40 to 45 problems on the computer.

In amazement, one teacher told her that, "With a pencil and paper, if I said that in this period we are going to deal with five problems, I would have a revolution on my hands. The thing about computers is that they *love* it. When they leave, they still want more."

In the past, Akron St. Vincent had never ranked among the top five schools in the Cleveland Diocese in English, mathematics or anything else. Soon, with the computer lab, St. Vincent was ranked in the top five in several subjects every year. This can be attributed to the tremendous power of computer learning to advance students at their own pace.

Although Robinson school was headed by a wonderfully dedicated principal, Ray Marshall, progress took longer, in part because of inertia, in part because our gift bought only half the terminals needed for the larger school. The rest were purchased with Title I funds several years later.

Eventually, the Robinson school also made tremendous strides by using the computer labs, and with that success I was able to arrange software demonstrations at the Akron School Board. When I was urged by a teacher to just give her school $150,000 "and we'll decide what to do," my answer was that what her school was doing wasn't working and I wanted to pay for something that would. I was not surprised by the resentment of me in the room. I was surprised when, despite the success of St. Vincent, no other schools in the Catholic Diocese moved to adopt computer labs.

That was when I decided that private schools needed competition as much as public schools. That was when I began thinking even more seriously about school choice.

In 1993, we started the Inter Faith Elementary School in Akron. We opened the school early and remained open late to provide before-and-after school care. This was the lab for developing the approaches to better serve inner-city urban children.

8. The Political Real World

In 1990, Ohio became the fifth state to enact statewide open enrollment. Under the law, schools must accept students from within their district and, providing space is available, may accept students from other districts, with the money following the child. In 1987, a similar law had been passed just for metropolitan Cleveland.

In December 1992, the Governor's Commission on Educational Choice, which I chaired, recommended two plans that would pilot school choice for consideration by the Ohio Legislature. Early in the year, State Rep. Bill Batchelder estimated to me there were only 25 votes for a scholarship program among the 99 members of the Ohio House.

By that time, I understood nothing would ever be tested unless something was done to change the political environment in Ohio. That something consisted of a concerted effort to raise money and elect legislators receptive to the idea of school choice, especially among Republicans. In my basic naïveté about the political process, I had earlier believed that demonstrating the solution to the problem to the right people would cause change.

My first dose of reality had come at an Akron School Board advisory committee. Our mission was to propose ways to improve K-12 education in Akron. There were 13 members, drawn primarily from the business community. Armed with the Buick story and information on vouchers that Ann had brought back from the Heritage Foundation, I proposed we recommend a voucher system for Akron.

I had anticipated opposition from groups with a vested interest in the status quo—public school administrators, teachers and union officials, but a second group emerged right there. These were the people who remembered the high quality of the public schools they had attended 30 to 50 years ago. Their first reaction was, "Why can't we just bring all the public schools up to standard?"

I laid out the voucher proposal. I explained the significance of empowering parents to choose the school for their children and of having the funding follow the student. The two co-chairs, Bob Mercer, Chairman of Goodyear, and Vern Odom, Executive Director of the Urban League, led the opposition. I lost the vote, eight to five. Looking back, I probably did well to get five votes.

In Republican Governor George Voinovich's victory in 1990, his party had taken only 38 seats in the House, although it did control the Senate. In the 1992 election, Republicans had increased in the House to 46, but were still the minority party. The Democrats had 53 seats.

It was clear to me that the general public wanted more school choice. Why didn't the Legislature reflect this mood?

From June 6 to July 5, 1994, the University of Akron Center for Urban Studies conducted a statewide public opinion poll which found that 89 percent of all Ohioans favored school choice and 72 percent favored public funding of a pilot school choice program.

Support was even stronger within the Ohio African American community, with 75 percent favoring a pilot program. The oft-repeated charge that support primarily was limited to Republicans was destroyed by the data: 77 percent of all Democrats supported a pilot program compared to 71 percent of Republicans.

Most surprising of all was the response of school employees. Nearly 65 percent said they would support "a grant program that permits public school districts to participate in short-term experimental projects in which grants would allow students to attend private, parochial, or alternative public schools."

When asked how they would likely vote if their district had an election to decide whether to participate in a school choice program, 53 percent said "yes." Perhaps most telling, 62 percent said that if their district had a grant program they would choose to participate in it.

Public dissemination of views like these might well have played a part in the House gains in the November 1994 elections. But so did a conversation I had had after the 1992 election.

Just after the election, I happened to meet with Vern Riffe. Vern was a Democrat and had been Speaker of the House for 22 years. To say Vern was politically savvy is a gross understatement. As Speaker, he would raise huge sums of money for his party. He would then dole it out where he felt it would do the most good.

In 1992, he had held back $2 million until 10 days before the election and then did daily polling to determine his best buys. In the final days, he bought the right advertising in the right districts while the Republican Party was out of money. In fact, we were broke.

His strategy was brilliant and successful. It may be standard practice now, but it was ingenious then.

Vern told me what he had done and I said, "That's incredible. Why don't we do that?" And Vern said he didn't know why we didn't.

In January 1993, I told two major Republican contributors from Cincinnati, Dick Farmer and Carl Lindner, what I had learned from Vern and said, "We've got to raise $2 million between now and next year. We will select 14 or 15 races and we will take back the House."

And that's what we did. Governor Voinovich coasted to victory with 72 percent of the vote, a 20th century record. Republicans now controlled the Senate, 20-13 and the House, 56-43. We also had the House leadership and committee chairs, elevating Mike Fox to chairman of the Education Committee where he could set the agenda for bills being called up and, in general, have a more formidable role in legislation than he had had in his preceding 20 years. Public hearings in 1994 in the Senate, under Senator Cooper Snyder's leadership, also had kept the recommendations of the Education Choice commission alive.

Along the way, I had become convinced that, no matter what the polls said, school choice would not be passed in a state-wide initiative. The common wisdom was that opposition was so well funded by the teachers' unions, we would be smothered. I had seen school-choice referenda fail elsewhere and decided not to waste money on a statewide vote in Ohio.

I had to chuckle when Cincinnati Federation of Teachers' President Tom Mooney charged in the December 7, 1994 *Cincinnati Post* that it was "outrageous" to attempt "to purchase" public policy with large campaign contributions to candidates who supported school choice, when the teachers' unions are the most powerful political force affecting legislation on education in Ohio and nationwide. Which they certainly are.

As to the unions' concern about students, I remember well when a leader in the Ohio Education Association, commenting on how the organization planned to spend a war chest of more than $4 million, said it would put its money on whatever side of the issue its leaders believed was in the best interest of their members. That organization has 117,000 members, and is part of the NEA, with 2.6 million members nationally.

Several years ago, the late Albert Shanker, president of the million-member American Federation of Teachers, expressed a similar sentiment when he said he would start representing students when students paid union dues.

A galvanizing factor to help move the Cleveland program to passage was added on March 3, 1995, when

U.S. District Judge Robert Krupansky directed the State Superintendent of Ohio to take immediate control of the Cleveland public schools. The district had been in decline for decades, a decline that nothing could seem to halt. Its debt, which had been $6 million in January 1990, was $140 million on the day Judge Krupansky handed down his decision.

At first in 1995, a proposal was introduced in the legislature that would have permitted any school district to vote in a scholarship program, with a state commission on choice created to select up to three districts for state-funded pilot projects. In Representative Fox's words then, the education establishment went "ballistic and we started to take on water." He and his fellow choice advocates would try "to figure out how we could pare this down to something doable."

Something doable was the Cleveland plan. What had developed as the wealthy and middle class had fled to the suburbs, in his estimation was, he told me, a case of "urban genocide," a contemporary "version of the plantation." In Cleveland, the failure of the system was so clear, he said, "We were on the side of the angels."

"I'm not trying to force legislation. I'm trying to save the children," Cleveland Councilwoman Fannie Lewis, a Democrat from Hough, told the *Toledo Blade* on March 5, 1995 as she led 300 inner-city Cleveland parents to a statehouse rally in Columbus.

Ohioans, meanwhile, had been watching Wisconsin which, in 1990, had created a 5-year program in the Milwaukee school district. Statistics over its first four years showed that 75 percent of the participating parents were single; 57 percent received federal Aid to Families with Dependent Children; more than 90 percent of the youngsters were eligible for the free lunch program; and 93 percent were minorities—74 percent African American and 19 percent Hispanic.

On June 22, 1995—just days before the Ohio legislature finally enacted the Cleveland program—despite the fact its program was being challenged in the courts, the Wisconsin legislature not only voted to renew it but increased the number of eligible students from one percent of total enrollment (about 1,000 students) to 7,000 for the coming school year and 15,000 for the next. It also authorized private religious schools to participate, adding some 50 new schools from which students could select.

Rep. Bill Batchelder had rewritten the Cleveland program legislation for the Governor following the Governor's request to be sure it did not conflict with the First Amendment of the United States Constitution.

The Governor had called me and told me that, if necessary, he was ready to go to war on the issue. "We're going to have choice in Ohio." It was included in the budget bill and it passed in the House. When it did not pass in the Senate, it went to Conference Committee where both the House and the Governor insisted it stay in.

Governor Voinovich's administrative aide for education was Tom Needles. He and I were in frequent communication. Tom became more and more committed to the cause, and today is our primary liaison with the Ohio legislature. His support has been invaluable.

On June 28, the budget bill passed 82-17 in the House and 29-3 in the Senate. Fifty-two of 56 House Republicans had voted for it, as did 30 of 43 Democrats led by Representative Patrick Sweeney of Cleveland. In the Senate, all 20 Republicans voted for it, as did nine of 13 Democrats, one being absent. Governor Voinovich signed the bill into law two days later.

In the House, the opponents had tried to strike the Scholarship Plan from the budget bill. The final vote on the motion was 57 to 42, including seven Democrats in our favor led by Patrick Sweeney.

Initially, the program would be available for students in kindergarten through the third grade. Each year after, one grade would be added up to and including the eighth grade. Students would not be required to stay in the same school from year to year, but could transfer.

If a student should drop out of the program for any reason, the scholarship would not be renewed. The Cleveland schools would keep all the state aid per pupil (an average then of $5,600) even if the maximum voucher amount ($2,250) was used.

Parents and families, empowered by choice scholarships, could leave any school that performed poorly.

All private schools needed to be state chartered and regulated by state standards.

Additional oversight would be mandated by the Ohio Department of Education, with the Cleveland office verifying residence and income and regulating all admissions standards.

The State Auditor of Ohio would monitor the fiscal accountability of the program.

We had lost in piloting choice on a wider scale, but we had succeeded in getting choice where it was most needed. We could not get beyond Cleveland to the other inner cities for one fundamental reason: Nearly all their House members were Democrats, funded by the teachers' unions, the most powerful political force this country has ever seen. Even when the industrial unions were at their peak of power, they never had such wealth. So if I'm a Democrat, what am I going to do—vote against my supporters?

The Republicans are generally elected from the suburbs and the rural areas. To this day, we have Republican dominance in areas where choice doesn't exist; but also where it's perceived as being not needed. If we could test vouchers in only one place, at least we did it where it was most needed. And the Democrats, no longer in control of the Ohio General Assembly, could not stop it.

9. The Indomitable Bert Holt

During World War II, our country missed its great opportunity to truly integrate our society. In the military, particularly in battle, people make friends for life. In a foxhole, social strata and racial and religious differences disappear. If African Americans had been integrated into the U.S. military during the Second World War, we would have saved our nation all these years of grief. It was a great mistake. We had the opportunity.

After I chaired his commission, Governor Voinovich gave me an award for my work in education. Six Tuskegee Airmen, the black flying outfit of that war, were being honored at the same time because at one time they had been based at Wright-Patterson in Dayton. I had the privilege of sitting next to one of them. I asked him, "As badly as black people had been treated, why did you fly for your country?"

"Because," he answered, "we knew one day we would win. We knew one day it would change." He was talking not just about winning the war. He was talking about winning the war against segregation in the South and against racism in America. He knew one day his country would change.

Very few African Americans I know who are my age, in all walks of life, are not privately bitter about how they were treated. Their children, the second generation, were able to escape the small Southern towns or the urban Northern ghettos because of the pioneering work of their parents.

Government deserves a lot of credit for this, for it provided the employment for many black people from my generation and from the next. The grandchildren, the third generation, men and women in their twenties and thirties who now live primarily in the suburbs, are the first generation that does not have to look back. They can give back. And it is from this age group that so many of the teachers in voucher schools and charter schools are coming.

I celebrate these young African-American teachers in the same way I celebrate the Tuskegee Airmen. Not because the Airmen did not lose one bomber to enemy aircraft in 200 escort missions. Not just because of their exploits as warriors, shooting down 111 Luftwaffe planes. But because the Airmen were, and the teachers are, pioneers for their own people.

Mrs. Bert Garrett Holt is one particular woman who bridges the generations between the Tuskegee Airmen and the young African-American teachers, and her story is a compelling chapter in the school choice movement.

In the late 1940s, the Garrett family lived on the campus of a small state college in West Virginia, where Bert's father taught science and her mother taught school. Mrs. Garrett had begun teaching in the segregated system of Paris, Kentucky while her husband, George, attended graduate school. The black schools there were separate, but hardly equal. Black students received textbooks and equipment only after white students had used and discarded them. Bert's mother persistently pressed the school administration for better opportunities for her students, and often succeeded. She taught Bert to strive for opportunity for her race and that the door to opportunity was the schoolhouse door.

Bert went to college, graduated with honors, and moved to Cleveland in the 1960s for her first teaching job. New school buildings rose then throughout the city. Academic excellence was a standard.

The schools were not perfect. Segregation troubled the system and the souls of many people, but the schools engaged the community. In 1963, Bert's husband, a second lieutenant in the U.S. Army, was assigned to France. Her first child was born there, her second after the family returned to Cleveland. When she returned, Bert taught social studies at Alexander Hamilton Middle School and later become chairperson of the department.

She expanded her students' knowledge of their world through her experiences in Europe. They not only understood the geography of the nations, they could tell each nation's national product. As she interested them in the rest of the world, her black students began to entertain thoughts of their heritage. She and the children's parents raised the money for a trip to five African nations, and "An African Odyssey" became a public television documentary.

In the 1970s, as in so many other big cities, urban unrest and racial conflict polarized Cleveland. Court ordered bussing wiped out the familiar and functional neighborhood schools. Families of all colors fled to the suburbs to smaller, more stable, communities and community-managed schools. Bert found herself in the eye of the storm working as an administrator for the Cleveland schools in the desegregation office.

Bert's job was to try to keep people believing in the system. She worked to build bridges between local business leaders, colleges and universities, the media and the public schools. While desegregation yielded some benefits for Cleveland's children and helped break down some barriers, marginal success came at a price. It was then, as Bert recalled to me later, she witnessed a dramatic change in priorities in public education. "It used to be that children came first," she told me, "but things began to slide seriously and the system lost focus. The vision for educating children as the first priority disappeared."

Due to the federal desegregation lawsuit, the operation of the Cleveland school district came under authority of the federal courts. The struggle over the Remedial Order to bring equality of educational achievement to all children in a desegregated setting overshadowed the education of children. Federal and state dollars flowed to transportation costs. Huge amounts were spent for lawyers, legal suits and, in my estimation, a bloated bureaucracy.

The teachers' unions ascended. Now the local school board had to deal with the courts, the lawyers, and hardball union tactics. The district was unable to pass a single school operating levy for 25 years.

In 1995, Bert tendered her resignation from the Cleveland public schools. She left with a clear conscience that she had done her best for Cleveland's children, and with profound respect from the educational community. She had several offers in the private sector and was moving toward a decision when a call came from the Ohio Department of Education.

The Ohio Legislature had passed a pilot plan to bring school choice to the Cleveland Public School System.

Why Cleveland? Because it was the largest system in the worst condition of the 611 school districts in the state. Legislators, despairing over years of failed attempts to help the Cleveland schools, had finally yielded to school choice leaders, and to the governor, and had passed a limited pilot plan. Nothing else had worked, so why not try choice.

Education leaders in Cleveland showed little to no enthusiasm. Per pupil expenditures in Cleveland were higher than the vast majority of other districts. Though the system was failing the children, it remained the biggest employer in town. The teachers' union hated the idea of choice. The Department of Education, though responsible by legislative mandate for running the program, was no more enthusiastic. So who could officially oversee the establishment of a school choice program in Cleveland? Bert Holt.

Bert said "Yes" for one simple reason. She believed this could be a remarkable opportunity for the children of Cleveland. It was November 1995.

The official director of the Ohio school-choice plan, Bert Holt, had three telephones in her office and a card table for a desk. She called a former seventh grade student with whom she had kept in contact for a lifetime. The student was now a successful human resources director for a major college. In a few days, Bert had an information systems manager and an administrative assistant ready to go to work.

Some 7,000 parents applied to that initial public offering. In January 1996, a lottery granted the first 2,000 of the highly coveted scholarships. From February to May, Bert's staff had to verify the scholarship recipients, help them find a school, register them with the program and process endless paperwork. Everything had to be ready for school to open in September.

Just to make matters a little more complicated, the ACLU and the teachers' unions filed suit to attempt to stop the plan. Weeks before school was to open, some 2,000 students and their parents did not know if they would be able to begin the program on time. A favorable court decision was granted and the doors of school choice were ready to open.

Bert expected buses for those 2,000 kids. But days before school was to open, she was told the Ohio Department of Education planned to provide payment instead. Few parents had adequate transportation, so Bert met with David Adams, who did all the routing for Cleveland schools; and they met with the Cleveland taxicab companies. On Monday, August 26,

1996, nearly 1,000 children were picked up and delivered by cab to school. Over the week, the rest were phased in.

Some of our opponents were in shock. We were supposed to have gone down in flames. Not having buses could have put us out of business. But not with Bert Holt. The day school opened, and throughout the following weeks, she was there to welcome the poorest children in Cleveland to a world of new opportunity.

10. Daring to HOPE

When I look back, sometimes I don't know how we did it. It seemed that every day an event would occur that threatened to shut us down.

The bill had been signed into law on June 30, 1995, providing 14 months of preparation for the private schools and 14 months of stalling tactics by the opposition. I didn't expect the Ohio Department of Education or the Cleveland Public Schools to publicize the program, so I formed "HOPE for Cleveland's Children" to do it myself. We distributed information describing the program. We produced two 30-second public service announcements. Our first organizational meeting was in August 1995. HOPE spent $150,000 in private funds to inform parents and encourage applications in 1995 and 1996.

By September 1995, the education department still had hired no one to head the program, nor had an administrative budget been established. Initially, applications had to be in by December 1. The deadline was extended to February 28, 1996.

Meanwhile, in November 1995, the redoubtable Bert Holt had been hired. In testimony later before a committee of the United States Congress and before the

Ohio House of Representatives, she would define school choice as "the unique emancipating opportunity for the urban poor."

By October, we were hearing that several people in the School Board office were misdirecting or misinforming callers. A memo went out to Superintendent John Goff, with a copy to Tom Needles in the Governor's office, noting that Cleveland's non-public schools had not received any notification of the program from the DOE. We offered a draft communication, and urged that day-care centers and Head Start providers be included in the mailing, since many youngsters in their care would be eligible for kindergarten in the fall. We emphasized that this information should be sent immediately.

We also discovered that the Department of Education had made an internal decision to limit the maximum tuition to $2,000. We got it reversed and it went back to $2,500.

We hired a local clergyman to help us provide information to the community. But, after less than a month, he resigned under pressure from peers opposed to the program. In many of the churches, a substantial amount of revenue was coming from the tithes of public-school teachers. Even church pastors were quick to learn the economics of maintaining government schools.

By December 1995, with Bert in place for less than two months, 5,700 children had applied and more applications were coming in.

The *Cleveland Plain Dealer* editorialized that the program had "already proved a key point. City parents do care about education." Recognizing a court suit was on its way, the editorial went on to say that "to pursue court action now, in the face of such enthusiasm, would not only alienate parents but would also harm the very children the public school advocates claim to protect. Let this experiment proceed. Measure its merits on the basis of educational results, not lawyers' arguments. Cleveland students deserve a chance and a choice."

Under guidelines established by the office of the Superintendent of Public Instruction, only students from families at or below the poverty line originally had been eligible for the scholarships. I believed then and still do that the intent was to scuttle the program, as these families would be least able to pay the required 10 percent of the tuition. Thanks to Bert, however, and as permitted by statute, provided those at or below the poverty level were accepted first, the program was opened to families at twice the poverty level, a group known as the "working poor."

On January 6, 1996, 1,500 scholarship winners each received a letter explaining they could attend any of 52 approved private schools in the city. The letter stated there would be a series of informational hearings with prepaid parking and bus tickets to make attendance easier. A form was distributed naming the available schools. Parents could indicate up to six schools in preferential order and admission would be based upon available space.

That same month, the American Federation of Teachers filed its lawsuit to challenge the program's constitutionality and asked for an injunction to stop it. Governor Voinovich issued a statement decrying the suit, saying, "It is inconceivable that a teachers' union would assume to know more about what is right for a child than the child's parents. It is a government's responsibility to empower parents with the right to choose where their children attend school." The Governor concluded that he would "vigorously fight to defend our program."

Some journalists were even harsher than the Governor in their criticism. One columnist said the teachers' union lawsuit would "sabotage the educational ideals it pretends to promote."

Appropriately, Representative Mike Fox, who had fought for choice through all his years in the legislature, made the reference that stood out most in my mind. "In 50 years," he said, "roles have been reversed in the Civil Rights movement. In 1957, Alabama Governor George Wallace stood in the schoolhouse door to block two black children from enrolling in the school of their choice. Today the education establishment stands at the schoolhouse door blocking the exit."

The day before the lawsuit had been filed, the state's ninth-grade proficiency tests were released. In Cleveland, only 10 percent of ninth graders had passed the math portion and only 25 percent had passed the reading test. This contrasted with 61 percent and 82 percent respectively in Parma, a suburb of Cleveland.

On July 31, 1996, Judge Lisa Sadler of the Franklin County Common Pleas Court denied the injunction and ruled the program constitutional under both the Ohio Constitution and the First Amendment of the United States Constitution. That's when our opponents promptly appealed and sought a restraining order. On August 12, the county Appeals Court unanimously denied the request for an injunction, but accepted the case for review. For now, the program could continue.

We had organized the HOPE program in August 1995. To promote the program and, when it was clear 350 more students would accept scholarships than could find places, we established two schools. When the appeal for the injunction was turned down, we started from scratch to open them. That day we hired our first two employees other than our administrator, Ann Yarman: John Morris as principal of both Hope

Central Academy and Hope City Academy, and Holly Bush as education director at Hope Central. We bought desks, chairs, and computers. We hired our teachers: some, from the public schools; some, substitutes without full-time jobs; some, college graduates who just wanted to teach; some, career women who decided to teach after their children were grown.

In early August 1995, Kevin Teasley and Fritz Steiger of the CEO America Foundation put together a golf outing at La Costa Golf Course in San Diego. Governor Voinovich was the main speaker, and I introduced him. More than 200 Hollywood actors, movie, and television people participated. At that event, I met John Walton of the Wal-Mart family for the first time. He told me his family foundation wanted to help us. Within days, the Walton Family Foundation committed $500,000 to the schools. The Brennan Family Foundation came up with a like amount.

The first order of business was to establish order itself. Incoming children had to learn how to behave before they could begin to learn. It took practice and perseverance. But within six weeks, John Morris was able to call the noise level in the halls a "sweet symphony." It also took six weeks for text books to arrive. "The amazing thing," John told me, was that the students already had learned "to focus on a task, reflect and respond to the instructor."

When we tested all our students, because we wanted to measure the effectiveness of our program and needed a base line, the results were far worse than even we expected. For instance, of forty third graders, only six performed at grade level and many could not even print their names. Over all, 32 percent of all our students performed at grade level, 58 percent needed remediation, and 10 percent needed special education. We hired a special education teacher, an art teacher, a music teacher, and a physical education teacher. We also hired tutors. By the middle of the school year, we were conducting after-school classes until 5 P.M. for about 40 children.

By late December, although there had been no formal testing, a self-assessment conducted by the teachers indicated that 50 percent could perform at grade level. By early 1997, while the Department of Education was still working on a process to evaluate the program, we had given our third-grade students the California Achievement Test twice, once in September 1996 and again in April 1997. In April, they scored five percentile points higher in reading and 15 percentile points higher in mathematical concepts than they had in September.

As the Heritage Foundation commented then, "This result is significant because test scores of poor minority students living in urban areas usually fall by one or two percentage points each year they are in school."

Parental involvement happened almost spontaneously. At times there were as many as 10 parents in a classroom. They also took it upon themselves to do what needed to be done, cleaning the buildings, working in the cafeterias. They helped the students understand the linkage between home and school. They were particularly helpful at the beginning and end of the day and at the lunch hour.

And who said the parents in the poorest families were not interested in their children? We had so many volunteers we hired assistants to manage their activity. Many of the parents received $5 an hour credit toward paying 10 percent of their tuition. A group of six men provided male guidance for many of the young boys. Each school had a Board of Directors and a Parents' Council that established their own bylaws.

We had developed a policy of total discipline and proper comportment. All students were required to wear uniforms to eliminate clothing competition. All children were to address any adult as "Sir" or "Ma'am." Naturally, we allowed no drugs or weapons of any kind. Any offensive behavior was immediately subject to corrective action.

In practice, virtually all problems were handled gently and effectively at the first instance by the teacher. In the entire first year of the Hope Academies, not one child was expelled from either school.

Parents of 55 of the 350 children in the academies did withdraw their children. The reasons, in general, had to do with curriculum or transportation. The fact that parents were free to do so should be seen as a success for school choice.

As for the arguments that vouchers would "cream" the best students from the public schools, leaving them with problem students, the truth is that a disproportionate number of youngsters who are from low income families, have disadvantage "problems," or have special needs, are the ones who leave the public schools for available alternatives. Actual practice in Cleveland and elsewhere revealed what common sense could have predicted.

Further impetus to school choice came on March 24, 1997 when the Ohio Supreme Court, in *DeRolph v. the Board of Education*, by a 4-3 margin, found Ohio's system of state funding of public education to be unconstitutional. The majority told the General Assembly that it must create "an entirely new" school financing system. "By our decision today, we send a clear message to lawmakers: The time has come to fix the system. Let there be no misunderstanding. Ohio's public school financing system must undergo a complete system overhaul."

That overhaul still waits.

Ohio Attorney General Betty Montgomery toured Hope Central in the same month, March 1997. She sent a thank you note to Principal Morris, saying, "I was very impressed," with "very" underlined twice. As a member of the Ohio Senate, she originally had not been in favor of the program. As Ohio Attorney General, her job came to entail defending school choice against court challenges. This required her to become much more deeply acquainted with the issues. As a result, she became a strong ally of the Cleveland plan.

I must say I liked the way Sol Stern, in the winter 1998 *City Journal*, described that year: that "under tough battlefield conditions," we were "able to offer a real-life demonstration of (the) theory that open markets and freedom from bureaucratic constraints will work wonders in education....Like the other voucher schools I visited, Hope Central Academy was living proof that professional certification and graduate education degrees are not synonymous with better educators."

11. Civility and Safety

By 2000-2001, there were 3,743 scholarship students and 1,271 tutoring students in the Cleveland Scholarship and Tutoring Program. The average scholarship value was $1,660. The cost to the average Ohio taxpayer was approximately $1.50.

The average school tuition in the program was $1,800 per student. The law permits public schools contiguous to the Cleveland School District to participate. To date, all neighboring districts have refused to accept scholarship students. The program expanded to nearly 5,000 students K-8 during the 2001-2002 academic year.

Meanwhile, the unions continued to argue there is no evidence that vouchers work. As Mathew Miller wrote in the July 1999 *Atlantic Monthly*, "that's a nervy case to make when it is union opposition that has kept the trials small."

Voucher antagonists also continued to argue that profit is bad and argue even louder today about profit and the charter movement. If there were no chance for a profit at all, who but the extravagantly wealthy or the public school systems themselves could afford to follow the path of operating charter schools?

In a March 2002 article in *Columbus CEO* magazine, a charter school dean, Greg Brown of the Graham School, spoke eloquently for himself, and for all dedicated people in the school choice movement. "No one goes into education to get rich," he said, "It's draining, exhausting work. But at the end of the day I feel like I've been involved in the heart of living....There's a sense of responsibility and doom—what happens if this thing fails? Who would we let down? It is almost intoxicating to be a part of something so meaningful."

Greg Brown is an alumnus of The Ohio State University, my undergraduate alma mater and the university on whose Board of Trustees I just served a nine-year term. The Graham School is *not* managed by my company. It is supported by a charitable trust. It is only two years old, already has a long waiting list and has purchased two more buildings. It is an innovative school, stressing community service.

To be chartered in Ohio, a school must be in a district under "academic emergency." That means the district has failed at least 21 of 27 standards of the State Department of Education.

The charter schools that thrive, I believe, will be the most innovative, like the Graham School. Innovation can come in simple ways. Uniforms are innovative. It is a sad comment on our times that two of the most attractive innovations a school can offer may be civility and safety.

How do you create civility in a school? The same way you do it at home. But you must start in the youngest grades. There are rewards and punishments for behavior. Everyone gets it wrong: Concentration is on punishment, not the reward. If you concentrate on the rewards, you have a civil pupil. Civility cannot be taken for granted. There must be a reward for civility.

We now use a system called "Champs." Champs is a classroom procedure whereby every time a student does anything in a classroom that lets his or her presence be known, even in misbehavior, three positive strokes follow in the next three minutes.

People are stunned at the time frame. How can that be done in the next three minutes? "David, your conduct a moment ago was out of line. You are such a fine boy and I know you'll never do that again because it hurts you and it hurts me." Forty seconds later, "David, I like the way you're sitting in that chair. You decided you are going to be a different kind of boy for the next few minutes." Ninety seconds later, "David, not only are you acting in a way that I like, look around you; your classmates do, too."

Champs was developed at the University of Oregon and, yes, not all teachers want to do this. In our schools, it's very simple. If they do not, they go work somewhere else.

Safety is the whole environment of the school. Safety among the children follows civility. If children are civil to each other, there are no terrible fights. Parents are most concerned about other kids beating up their kids. Safety to them is not someone coming in off the street with a rifle. But we have put off-duty uniformed police in our Cleveland grade schools anyway. We have had no incidents. Our neighbors have been very supportive.

White Hat no longer runs voucher schools. Some White Hat charter schools are elementary and middle schools. Some are high schools. I have found that what my company really does best is serve high school dropouts and those at risk of dropping out. We call those programs "Lifeskills." More about that in a moment.

12. Lifeskills Centers

An extraordinary phenomenon has occurred in my lifetime. In the '30s and '40s, the Republican Party was a very conservative, big-business, free-enterprise, pure-capitalism group of people who fought every program we would now call the safety net.

They fought Social Security; they fought Unemployment Compensation; they fought Medicaid. (They did not fight Workers' Compensation only because it benefited business. It prevented employees from suing their employer.) The Republican arguments in opposing the programs were, first, we could not tax ourselves enough to pay for them. Secondly, the programs would foster citizen dependency on the government and, thus, destroy individual initiative.

First, I reluctantly acknowledge that the liberals proved the point that we can afford those programs and still prosper. The government is the logical entity to collect funds and make sure the safety net exists and helps people. But the government should not be the sole dispenser of the service. I am of the school very much for the safety net, but for using the private economy to deliver the service.

Second, I suggest the liberals lost the second argument: We *have* created mammoth dependency on government. Welfare reform is the first recognition of this fact. Further privatization of government service is necessary, beginning with education.

The Democratic and Republican Parties also reversed roles. The Democrats are the party of the computer and high-tech firms. And they are defending the institutions, primarily the unions and government employees, against attacks on their job security and their future, just as the Republicans defended big business in the past.

And now what is happening? The Republicans are saying maintaining the safety net is the right thing to do, but with the caveat that we should have individual empowerment within it to reduce dependence upon government.

Did I wake up one morning and say, "Education is where I want to spend the rest of my life?" No, I did not. But I woke up one morning and realized I had lived past 55. Everything of meaning, everything that has to do with why I am here, except my marriage and my children, has happened since then.

My father had convinced me I would be dead at 55. He was a Type II diabetic. He had other illnesses, and he had heart disease from the time he was 55. Although he lived to 64, his last three years were spent in and out of the hospital.

In 1947, I went back with him to Boston to visit a famous doctor, Paul White, who later became the physician for President Eisenhower. He was the first physician of note who suggested heart patients should walk and exercise. Prior to Paul White, you stayed in bed and waited to die. Dr. White told my dad, "Of course, your son will have the same diseases." And he and my dad agreed I would probably not see 50, and I definitely would not live beyond the age of 55. I was 17. It was a conversation I should never have heard.

If you were born in 1900, your life expectancy was 47. Both my father and Dr. White were men who lived through this time and thought 55 was a pretty good age. Medicine was just acknowledging degenerative diseases—high blood pressure, enlarged heart, diabetes, heart condition problems—and saying they were inherited and irreversible. I would have Type II diabetes, and would have high blood pressure; thus, if there were to be heart surgeries in medicine's future, I could never be a candidate.

My father lived less then two more years. We had a special relationship and I attribute my success to it. He loved people and he appreciated people, and he taught me nobody is beneath friendship. But I lived until 43 on a fast track, believing my time was limited.

By 43, I was terribly overweight, my high blood pressure was out of control, diabetes was acting up and my heart was enlarged. Then, in January 1975, I went to the Duke University Medical Center. A man I knew named Freddy Myers had lost 48 pounds there on the rice diet. And if Freddy could do it, so could I. I went on the rice diet, was there for nine weeks, and saved my life.

I lost 65 pounds. By the time I left, my blood sugar, heart size, and blood pressure were all normal. The last day there I won the dance contest with a woman who, a year before, had been admitted in a diabetic coma. I was shown I could reverse these non-reversible diseases. It was not common wisdom, and I became a believer.

For the next 25 years, I ate rice and tomato sauce. I would go into a restaurant with my plastic container of rice and tomato sauce in a paper bag, and say, "Heat this up for me." I made it the most important thing in my life. I struggled with that diet for 25 years—until three years ago, slowly taking weight off, then gaining it back, then losing it again.

I went on another diet for diabetics, developed by Dr. Richard Bernstein. It is basically pure protein, and I have fared very well on that.

Through this all, I learned what is important in life is how I live, and how I feel about how I live. What drives me, what I want to see happen, is some kind of solution for these inner-city kids being left behind. That drives me like an engine. Out of that concept, all sorts of spillover effects are occurring. Mostly intended, some unintended. Mostly expected, some not expected. The real point is, whether I win or lose financially is immaterial in the sense I'm going to be driven to do this until the day I die.

One out of three Ohio high school students does not get a diploma.

Three years ago, we began opening charter high schools for dropouts. We call them Lifeskills Centers. They are modeled after the Learning Centers in the company plants, which proved so effective. They are open to dropouts age 16 to 22.

Last year, 150,000 Ohio children became 18 and, of those, 50,000 will never graduate from high school. In this state alone, in the 16 to 22 age group, non-graduation creates 350,000 candidates for minimum

wage jobs or, at best, 350,000 candidates educational-
ly inadequate for the twenty first century. Could it be
we are doing something wrong? Isn't it possible we
could do better?

Ohio is no longer a state, nor is the Midwest a region,
where hundreds of thousands of high school dropouts
can make a good living on the assembly line. Ohio
used to be near the top in per capita personal income.
Now we are 22nd and falling.

In Lifeskills, the academic day is only four hours.
Three hours are computer instruction. The fourth is
"life skills" instruction. Students who already have a
job do not have to be there the fourth hour. A
Lifeskills graduate earns a high school diploma, not a
GED. In Lifeskills, students educate themselves.
When they need help, they seek and get it. They are
not listening to some teacher blather on while they're
half asleep and not tuned in. For them, the traditional classroom with a teacher at the head of the class
was the most inefficient delivery system educators
could create.

Walk into our Akron center and you walk into an
area that has four pods. Each pod has up to 50 computer work stations. Normally that pod will be filled
with 35 to 50 students. Each pod has three fulltime

teachers and two aides. We fill those seats four times a day in three-hour blocks between 8 A.M. and 9 P.M.

We stagger the work shifts. An employment counselor and social worker works with each group. We now require 60 percent attendance to stay in school, and I expect to increase that to 80 percent. This is a vocational school and they get credit for work time. We are in our third year and soon will have 15 centers operating. We already have 1,000 graduates as of December 2001, and I have every reason to believe we soon will be teaching 12,000 students in Ohio.

High school teachers complain they have no time to be one on one with students, to really help deal with the lives of young people. In Lifeskills we do that beautifully. Teachers have incredible personal relationships with the students. What we have done is transform the teacher from a teacher to a manager of the learning process. Two-thirds of the work load is carried by the student, not the teacher. We have made the teacher three times as productive. It isn't rocket science. I realized recently that we may be designing the high school of the twenty-first century.

Some of the smartest students, bored to tears in high school, have figured that, as they enter their junior year, they can drop out, go to Lifeskills in November and graduate in June. "I get two years done by June." And they can. They've figured it out.

Lifeskills students have to wear "uniforms," Lifeskills tee-shirts and dark pants or skirts. They will conform that much.

Some have dropped out for as long as three years. They find out about this program through word of mouth. About a third of them have drug or alcohol problems. The program doesn't do any good if they can't pass a drug screening test. How can we help with that?

There is nothing more effective than the mutual help of caring, loving people. These kids are young and I call most of them "shallow addicts." They have only abused substances for a year or two. We don't yet have a program, but we soon will. The 12-step program of the AA works. We are going to emulate it, probably through a five-step program. We are going to make it happen.

This is what we do best. This is where I know I can do the most good now. Some educrats claim we are taking money away from them because the money is channeled through the school districts. So they hate us. But the teachers are beginning to send us students.

Let the student be a learner. What a wonderful concept. It is how Oxford has thrived for centuries. And we seem to have decided, "No, everything must come through the golden chords of some highly paid professional." What a bunch of rubbish!

To date, we are graduating 50 percent of our regular attendees per year, better than many school districts. All of them want a job. Eighty-five percent so far have become employed.

13. Charter Schools

This book has been primarily about how the Cleveland Scholarship and Tutoring Program came to be, and the forces that drove school choice in Ohio. It has also, however, been about school choice nationally; about school choice as a greater good for children.

When I chaired Ohio Governor George Voinovich's Commission on Educational Choice in 1992, we were not there to debate whether choice was good or bad. Rather, having accepted that something should be done, we were there to decide what that something should be.

Eventually, the Commission's work spawned the Cleveland program. And today in Ohio we have alternative schools, magnet schools, home schooling, "virtual" or on-line schools, the voucher pilot in Cleveland and, in districts declared by the Ohio Department of Education in "academic emergency," charter or "community" schools.

I have written already about charter schools operated by our company. Charter schools are created through a contract (a charter) with a statutorily designated agency to operate under express conditions. Given the opportunity to innovate, they must achieve certain goals to justify their existence.

In Ohio, we must either exceed public school test scores or increase ours at least 2.5 percent per year. Charter schools are not permitted to teach religion. (See Appendix B for the similarities and differences between voucher and charter schools.)

In 1999, there were 75,000 students in the Cleveland public school district. Of these, 18,000 went to magnet schools. In addition, 2,000, or so, were enrolled in community (charter) schools, 3,700 accepted scholarships to use in sectarian schools, and another 100, or so, in non-sectarian schools. Another 1,400 took advantage of the tutorial program. At one time, there were more non-sectarian schools available, but two of the major ones closed. Later, two community schools opened in the same building.

This was part of Solicitor General Ted Olson's testimony on February 20, 2002 before the United States Supreme Court in *Zelman v. Simmons-Harris*. The two major school locations now managed as community (charter) schools had been Hope Academies. As Dave Young already had pointed out, "when (the Cleveland) program was initially implemented, every single secular school in the district signed up to participate (as a voucher school). Additionally, two brand-new secular schools were established by reason of this program, the two HOPE schools. They remained in the program until the Community School Act was adopted. That, indeed, doubled the amount of money available to the families. In other words, the maximum grant (was) $2,250— but, if the same children elected to go to a community school, the State would pay for each child at least double the amount that it would pay if they selected the scholarship."

"(That) the Sixth Circuit refused to consider the community schools is beyond me," he added in answer to a justice's question. And it is beyond me, as well. As Justice O'Connor said when Robert Chanin argued that only the voucher option was the "reality" of this case, "You're asking us to look at *part* of a reality."

When the argument was made that community (charter) schools should not be considered as different from the traditional public school, one justice noted that the public school system "that failed" was the traditional public school system, and that the charter schools "are basically private schools... getting a different kind of state aid."

Charter schools, of course, are funded directly by the state—which, in my opinion, is substantially inferior to funding via the hands and decisions of the consumer.

Witness the food stamp program, a most effective consumer-controlled but governmentally-administered choice plan. The federal government could have created commissaries to issue the food, but chose instead to give stamp recipients the opportunity to select from every grocery store and supermarket. That the quality of the delivery to *all* consumers is essentially the same, I believe, is the desired result of all such programs.

Why is consumer choice so important? Because, if the consumer goes elsewhere, the employees of the supplier could lose their jobs. Do not be misled; accountability cannot effectively be mandated by statute or regulation. The possibility of job loss is the only effective accountability measure. In any situation when the employee's job is protected even when the employee is not doing the job, there is no accountability for failure. This is why monopolies never satisfy their customers over the long haul. This is also why government service delivery is so often expensive and ineffective.

While many teachers unions' lobbyists oppose all types of school choice, they most intensely oppose the inclusion of religious schools. Rarely is this understood: Non-secular schools are not subject to jurisdiction by the National Labor Relations Board; none of the federal legislation that supports the rights of unions to represent employees applies to religious schools. The Supreme Court has ruled on numerous occasions that to permit this to happen would be an unnecessary entanglement with religion.

The net effect, of course, has been great difficulty organizing such teachers. Could this possibly be a principal reason some teachers unions' elites object so loudly to non-secular schools in the menu of choice?

The Netherlands has had school choice for approximately 75 years. In the beginning, virtually all students went to government schools. Today, only 25 percent of the students are in government schools and 75 percent are in non-government schools. Two-thirds of those non-government schools are religious schools. A very broad array of religions is represented in this menu of choice. It is fair to say that half the parents would prefer their children to be educated in a religious environment.

In 1992, the A.T. Kearney consulting firm, retained by the Ohio Commission on Educational Choice, projected that vouchers of $2,215 for grade school students and $3,971 for high school students might motivate as many as 45 percent of public school students to switch to private schools. At that time, the cost of educating a public school student in Ohio was $5,390.

The total statewide savings, according to the Kearney report, could have been as much as $600 million a year in 1992.

In her final rebuttal comments before the Supreme Court, Judith French, in arguing for choice, said that it was "apparent from the Court's questions and the respondents' arguments that the Ohio General Assembly had a number of competing and conflicting considerations before it in the face of and in an environment of an educational crisis it needed to solve, and to solve quickly.

"It seems," she concluded, "that Ohio did it right...."

In my opinion, any state that authorizes charter schools should also be willing to authorize voucher schools with the same economic benefits per pupil. It also would make sense that vouchers be for some lesser amount, perhaps 90 percent, in exchange for the right to charge tuition in addition to the voucher.

Tax credits are another way of funding vouchers, but the effect is essentially the same. In short, voucher schools are easier to establish than charter schools, have less state regulation, and are very responsive to parental pressure. While both are operating in Milwaukee, demonstrating a market for each, given the choice between vouchers and charters, all things being equal, I believe vouchers will prevail. Finally, to be able to fund vouchers for the existing private school students, funding should be phased in over six to eight years.

These ideas once were theory, at least as far as the twentieth century United States was concerned.

Now, because of work in Florida, Wisconsin and here in Ohio, we are learning what works best for children, parents and school systems. This work did not begin in Washington, D.C., nor will it end there.

The dream of all children to fulfill their God-given ability to learn is a quest for all generations.

14. A Pre-decision Epilogue

Some people get caught up in this kind of quest and it costs them dearly in a material sense. My observation has been that when all you want is wealth, you live a very empty existence: Because there's nothing there. Wealth doesn't care who owns it. Stock doesn't care who owns it. Real estate doesn't care who owns it.

I believe in the Biblical admonition: To paraphrase, you're supposed to maximize your talents. If you're a writer, be the best writer. If you're a programmer, be the best programmer. If you're a lawyer, be the best lawyer God can put on this earth. All the way down the line.

We, at White Hat, are very good at the things we do. I am obligated to keep doing those things for the rest of my life. My heart surgeon says I may now have another 20 years. How can I build on that? That is my next great adventure.

Carl Sagan had a wonderful example of the insignificance of the human species on the history of the earth. On a big stage, he placed a dozen or so large blackboards, and in the lower right hand corner of the last one he put a one inch square. That's the amount of time human beings have been on earth. Talk about insignificant. In the context of that, what I am doing is terribly insignificant. But I am beginning to believe, as an infinitesimal quark on that miniscule square, I am at least a positive force.

15. The Decision

"In sum, the Ohio program is entirely neutral with respect to religion. It provides benefits directly to a wide spectrum of individuals, defined only by financial need and residence in a particular school district. It permits such individuals to exercise genuine choice among options public and private, secular and religious. The program is therefore a program of true private choice. In keeping with an unbroken line of decisions rejecting challenges to similar programs, we hold that the program does not offend the Establishment Clause."

"The judgment of the Court of Appeals is reversed."

"It is so ordered."

The conclusion of the opinion of the Court, June 27, 2002

For more than a week, the Court had been issuing its rulings and, as we suspected, it saved *Zelman v. Simmons-Harris* for the last day. I was at home doing my physician-ordered exercises when Connie Marucco, my executive assistant, came into the house with the news. Tom Needles had called. Kim Kleine, spokesperson for the U.S. Department of Education, had phoned him. We had won. It was Thursday morning, June 27, 2002. The decision was 5-4. More calls began to come in. My workout was over.

James Vicini of Reuters, the international news services, told the world that day that the decision "could reshape American education." Education Secretary Rod Paige hailed it as historic. "In communities all across America," he told the *New York Times*, "thousands of parents are clamoring for more and better options for their children."

Within hours of the decision, Majority Leader Dick Armey introduced a bill in the House of Representatives to provide vouchers for families under 185 percent of the poverty level in grades K-12 in the District of Columbia. Here in Ohio, some of my legislative friends began to urge expansion of the Cleveland program to other cities. The *Times*, never a proponent of school choice, reported that recommendations for programs soon could surface in Arizona, Colorado, Minnesota, Texas and Utah. The *Christian Science Monitor*, a few days later (July 1) added California, Pennsylvania, and Florida to the list.

The morning following the ruling, the *Columbus Dispatch* ran a photo that told the human story better than "a thousand words," as did the *Monitor* on July 1. Rosa-Linda Demore-Brown, executive director of the Cleveland Parents of School Choice, and

Cleveland mother Roberta Kitchen, with two children receiving vouchers, had just heard the news. They were rushing toward each other, arms outstretched in celebration. Roberta's smile was broad as Lake Erie.

Below the *Dispatch* photo was a separate story out of Washington, bylined by Jack Torry, that I found most satisfying. It was a profile of my fellow Ohio State University alum Judi French. It quoted Walter Dellinger, Acting Solicitor General under President Clinton. Judi had led "the ultimate Cinderella team in the Supreme Court tournament," he said, and "walked away with the trophy." Given the challenge to her expertise before the case was argued, I am nearly as happy today for Judith French as I am for the country. Ohio Attorney General Betty Montgomery told Torry she had become so furious then, that impugning French's experience cemented her decision to stick with her.

Judi's preparation for the case was so thorough that, with Ken Starr and others, she had formally rehearsed her arguments eight times; a number, she said, otherwise "unheard of." Her earlier preparation at home included testing her walk to the lectern. While not an uncommon practice, her test walks were done to the soundtrack from *Gladiator*. Many times, also at home, she had argued the case before her young daughter, Julia.

16. The Majority Opinion

"We believe that the program challenged here is a program of true private choice, consistent with Mueller, Witters, and Zobrest, and thus constitutional. As was true in those cases, the Ohio program is neutral in all respects toward religion."

From "The opinion of the Court," delivered by Chief Justice William H. Rehnquist

The concurring Justices were Antonin Scalia, Clarence Thomas, Anthony Kennedy, and Sandra Day O'Connor. Dissenting were Justices David Souter, Stephen Breyer, Ruth Bader Ginsburg, and John Paul Stevens. As some people had predicted, this was the same split vote that had overturned the injunction and then agreed to hear our appeal. While I had hoped and prayed, I had never dared to predict.

In setting forth the reasons for the majority opinion, Justice Rehnquist affirmed a line of decisions, begun in 1983 with *Mueller v. Allen*, that hold "programs of true private choice in which government aid reaches religious schools only as a result of the genuine and independent choices of private individuals" to be constitutional.

In *Mueller,* the Court rejected an Establishment Clause challenge to a Minnesota program that authorized tax deductions for various educational expenses, including sectarian school tuition costs; in *Witters,* it rejected an Establishment Clause challenge to a vocational scholarship program that provided aid to a student studying to become a pastor; in *Zobrest,* it rejected an Establishment Clause challenge to a federal program that permitted sign language interpreters to assist deaf children in sectarian schools.

"Reviewing our earlier decisions," the Chief Justice wrote, "we stated that 'government programs that neutrally provide benefits to a broad class of citizens defined without reference to religion are not readily subject to an Establishment Clause challenge.'"

He also cited seven essential elements of the Ohio Plan that had caused him to conclude the Cleveland program is one of true private choice, and is thus constitutional.

- The plan is neutral in all respects toward religion.

- It is part of a general and multifaceted undertaking by the State of Ohio to provide educational opportunities to the children of a failed school district.

- It confers educational assistance directly to a broad class of individuals defined without reference to religion.

- It permits the participation of all schools within the district, religious or nonreligious.

- Public schools in adjacent school districts also may participate, and are eligible to receive the tuition grant as well as "the full amount of per-pupil state funding attributable to each additional student."

- Benefits are available to participating families on neutral terms, with no reference to religion.

- The lone preference stated anywhere in the program is given to low income families, who receive greater assistance and are given priority for admission at participating schools. (The Chief Justice specifically stated that features of this final item are not necessary to constitutionality.)

As to the *Committee v. Nyquist* case, which generated sustained questioning at the hearing, the Chief Justice wrote that in *Nyquist*, the Court "...expressly reserved judgment with respect to a case involving some form of public assistance, (that is, scholarships) made available generally without regard to the sectarian—non-sectarian or public—nonpublic nature of the institution benefited..."

It had been Justice O'Connor who had first asked whether ruling for *Zelman* would require overruling *Nyquist*, the 1973 case in which the Court had ruled unconstitutional a New York tuition assistance program just for private school students. As Linda Greenhouse of *New York Times* had written, Justice O'Connor had "pressed both sides" and expressed "some skepticism about the answers she received" on a number of issues. The answer she had received from Judi French about *Nyquist* was that it would not have to be overturned, which Judi then explained through questions by a number of justices. The majority agreed.

As the Chief Justice wrote in his decision, "To the extent the scope of *Nyquist* has remained an open question in light of these later decisions, we now hold that *Nyquist* does not govern neutral and educational assistance programs that, like the program here, offer aid directly to a broad class of individual recipients defined without regard to religion." This reasoning is particularly heartening and gratifying to me because the very issues of *Nyquist* were the ones considered by the drafters of the Ohio Plan.

Specifically, the Ohio Plan did fit into the exceptions referred to in *Nyquist*. All the Ohio Plan participants —the constitutional lawyers, the legislators, and advisors in the period of 1992 through 1995—deserve enormous credit for coming to a consensus on what such a plan should entail. The fact that the Court expressly so found demonstrates how careful planning in the context of existing decisions can result in successes elsewhere.

While knowing the other elements of the Cleveland voucher case may be important in understanding the process that eventually passed legislation in Ohio, the Court clearly expresses its view: The only two important constitutional tests are the ones referred to in the majority opinion. This is a very broad decision covering choice plans of every type and nature which, if they meet the two tests, will be considered constitutional by the current Court.

On the other hand, the dissenting opinions written by Justices Souter, Stevens, and Breyer clearly show that a swing of only one vote would have found the opposite result. Justice Souter particularly expresses the opinion that he cannot wait to have the opportunity to vote again on this issue. If he happens to be in the majority at that time, one need not wonder what his decision will be. Much important litigation is decided by only a one-vote margin. However, it should be many years before this question is considered again by the U. S. Supreme Court.

17. Justice O'Connor's Concurring Opinion

Many observers do believe the swing vote that created the majority in *Zelman v. Simmons-Harris* was Justice Sandra Day O'Connor's. Her acceptance of unconditional and partial parent choice has progressed through the cases cited by Chief Justice Rehnquist over the past 20 years. Her concurring opinion fully embraces the reasoning and conclusions of Chief Justice Rehnquist's opinion, but adds further thoughts important to understanding her decision.

As she wrote in her opinion, "I write separately for two reasons. I do not believe that today's decision, when considered in light of other longstanding government programs that impact religious organizations and our prior Establishment Clause jurisprudence, marks a dramatic break from the past. Second, given the emphasis the Court places on verifying that parents of voucher students in religious schools have exercised 'true private choice,' I think it is worth elaborating on the Court's conclusion that this inquiry should consider all reasonable educational alternatives to religious schools that are available to parents. To do otherwise is to ignore how the educational system in Cleveland actually functions."

When the Board of Trustees of HOPE Central Academy, a voucher school, and HOPE Tremont Academy, a voucher school, voted in the spring of 1999 to terminate their status as voucher schools, this action was highly criticized by many people in the school-choice movement. New boards were constituted of different directors who then proceeded to establish charter schools in the same physical locations.

The motivation for this decision came from parents' concern that there be an alternative school for their children in case the voucher program did not survive. The District Court and the Court of Appeals had just declared the Cleveland Plan unconstitutional and the future of vouchers was very much in question. Creating charter schools seemed to be the best approach to solve the problem for the children. In hindsight, that was indeed the case.

In her opinion, Justice O'Connor cites my Affidavit (Appendix D) about the effect of our voucher schools and the subsequent establishment of charter schools. She found it important that voucher applicants could find a school without being turned away, because our voucher schools provided sufficient openings to satisfy all applicants, and she found it just as important that community schools were available to continue this option for parents after the voucher schools closed.

It is gratifying that she refers to my affidavit three separate times in support of her conclusions. A fourth reference, to an evaluation of the Cleveland Voucher Program after two years, points to the "HOPE Academy schools" having "among the highest rates of parental satisfaction of all voucher schools, religious or otherwise...particularly impressive given that a Harvard University study found that the HOPE Academy schools attracted the 'poorest and most disadvantaged students.'"

It appears our decisions not only were good for the children, they played a significant part in Justice O'Connor's concurring decision.

18. What the States Should Do

Urban life throughout Europe is far more satisfactory than it is virtually any place in the United States. Many European families would prefer to live in the city, if they could: City life is exciting; activities are all within walking distance; generally the cost of living is less than in suburbia; and for many people, their home is close to work. European cities, like their American counterparts, have their problems, but there is no shortage of residents in most European downtowns. Their central cities grow or are stable, while American central cities, particularly in the Midwest, shrink as the suburbs bloat.

In my own state of Ohio, I have watched Youngstown, Akron, Cincinnati, Columbus, Toledo, Cleveland, and Dayton all lose much of their core populations, while the rings of affluence grow around them, and the suburban shopping centers draw more traffic and cash away from downtown. Yet I hear many people yearn for the excitement of urban life, and I see many single professionals move into the few downtown apartments and condos in some of these cities, only to flee to the suburbs once their children are born and schools become the issue. While the city leaders often pour money into arenas, ballparks, and other venues to attract downtown attendance—as they have in Cleveland, Columbus, and Cincinnati—prior to and following the events that take place there, the cities empty again.

There are many theories as to why European cities do not have the same population problems we do. My own is that in European cities schools are located everywhere: in apartment buildings, at work sites, in shopping centers, as well as in traditional school buildings. This wide array of choices carries with it substantial parental involvement and control over the schools' activities. In fact, if you ask Americans where they would like to live, their answer will, in one form or another, include the quality of schooling for their children or their grandchildren.

When we improve the quality of inner-city schooling, we can restore the vitality to American cities they enjoyed in previous generations, and school choice is the vehicle to do this. As evident in the Netherlands, where full school choice has been available for seventy-five years, 50 percent of the parents seem to prefer a religious environment for the education of their children. I believe the same percentage would apply in America. (Perhaps the visceral reaction to a district court's ruling against retaining "under God" in the Pledge of Allegiance exemplifies this as much as anything.) Charter schools are not enough, nor is choice among public schools going to be enough. A voucher plan for all is essential to successfully restore our cities.

As columnist David Broder wrote following the Court's decision, "the evident failure of many urban bureaucracies—the old welfare system being one notable example and the school system another—might well require traditional liberals to open their minds about the possibility of redrawing the lines between church and state."

It is obvious there is no clamoring for school choice in the suburbs and rural areas, where parents feel more in control of what is happening at their schools than in the cities. While it can be argued that the plight of the cities is as much an effect of the flight to the suburbs as anything else, it is politically foolish to try to establish choice where it is not wanted. Statewide failures of voucher proposals have verified this. If the success of choice schools becomes evident to suburbanites of the future, they can easily expand the opportunity to suburbs, as well. As some people speculate, this also may happen in individual schools if failures in proficiency testing expose certain problems. Regardless, it is very clear that choice is much needed in our cities, and, the sooner the better.

As Justice Clarence Thomas wrote in his concurring opinion, vouchers can rescue children from "inner city schools that deny emancipation of minority students....While the romanticized ideal of universal public education resonates with the cognoscenti who oppose vouchers, poor urban families just want the best education for their children, who will certainly need it to function in our high-tech advanced society." That, however, is only half the story.

I strongly recommend that Ohio, and other states, extend vouchers to everyone living within the school districts of urban America. While, as Kate Zernike recently wrote in the *Times*, the Supreme Court decision was "rooted in morality, not economics," economics is involved in regrowing our nation's cities as well as in helping current residents escape poverty or near-poverty. Thus, I believe vouchers should be available to the urban resident, not just to the urban poor.

We often reward businesses with tax abatements when they are willing to relocate and bring jobs into our cities. We should also reward individuals. I cannot think of a better way to increase middle-class involvement than to reward families who are living in the city, and also families who move into it, with school vouchers. To limit all voucher programs only to the urban poor will, I'm afraid, only increase further flight to the suburbs: As more current residents receive an education that will allow them to leave, they will probably do so. While we will have helped a generation of our poorest citizens, we will not have helped our cities. Both are not only admirable objectives; they are closely linked.

Because, for most families, housing and schooling are inexorably connected, providing vouchers to all households in a targeted district will substantially increase the move-in of middle-class families, who will want to select quality schools while paying much less for their homes.

At the very least, vouchers should be made available wherever charter schools are authorized. Again, I would limit this to the cities, for both plans, even though charters may be available in the suburbs. In exchange for the right to charge more tuition than provided by the voucher, I believe the voucher should be 90 percent of the amount of funding available at charter schools. The voucher plan could provide that poverty-level children attend a school in consideration of the voucher, plus no more than 5 percent in additional tuition. This would maintain greater support for public education than for private education, a minor factor in discussions of the Cleveland voucher case. Continuing and expanding public school choice, including magnet schools and alternative schools, also should be part of the choice menu for urban parents.

By removing the constitutional objection to vouchers, and having the state institute such programs for the urban areas, long-term plans can be made by families to continue or initiate their residency in the city. Until now, the uncertainty surrounding the Cleveland Scholarship and Tutoring Plan certainly created a chilling effect on parents' decisions, as well as decisions to expand vouchers to other urban centers. Because the Ohio Supreme Court previously decided the voucher plan does not violate the First Amendment, Ohio can and should foster such legislation. Unfortunately, however, in other states, opponents likely will try to litigate in state court to stop such plans.

In a recent decision, the Second Circuit Court of Appeals in Oregon determined that the *Zelman* case is the law of the land, and that an 1857 state constitution provision restricting attendance at religious schools with state dollars is unconstitutional. This is particularly noteworthy since that circuit is considered extremely liberal. It is following the basic legal concept that the U.S. Supreme Court makes the final decisions and those decisions are binding on the entire federal court system.

On the other had, in a very recent case (*Holmes v. Bush et al.*, Second Circuit Court, Leon County), a Florida circuit court decided that the *Zelman* case controls

Florida law for the purposes of First Amendment objections, but that the state's separate constitutional "Blaine Amendment," an 1885 provision, is controlling.

"Blaine Amendments" restrict the ability of a state to permit state funds to directly or indirectly find their way to religious institutions. They were born of anti-immigrant, anti-Catholic sentiment as a failed U.S. Constitutional amendment in 1875 to encourage attendance in public schools. To me, the Florida ruling is a clear violation of the express intentions and provisions of the Fourteenth Amendment*, and this case clearly will be reversed on appeal. It is an indication, however, of the direction opponents will continue to take in trying to stop voucher plans around the country.

I encourage legislatures to proceed in any event, because this is too important for the restoration of America's cities and for the benefit of our children. We should refer to those cities as Educational Empowerment Zones.

---

* "No state shall make or enforce any law which shall abridge the privileges or immunitites of the citizens of the United States..."

19. Federal Legislation

Because the U.S. Supreme Court's decision is binding on the entire federal court system, further federal litigation on this issue will not occur. In Ohio, where the Cleveland Plan had passed constitutional muster by the Ohio Supreme Court under the First Amendment, the opponents proceeded immediately to Federal Court to try to stop the Plan. That second leg of objection has now been removed for any school-choice plans started in other states. While that is not the entire solution, it is a substantial step forward.

However, since the constitutional barrier has been removed, Congress could now pass legislation by which all states could foster and improve the opportunities for parents. As an example, Title I funds and funds for disabled students now are disbursed through public school districts and find their inefficient way to non-public schools, usually in amounts much less than Congress appropriated. This case should encourage Congress to voucherize public school funds, and thus eliminate the bureaucratic way stations of public school districts, which administer funds that easily could be handled directly by the intended beneficiaries.

Title I monies are made available to students on free or reduced lunch programs, and average up to $1,500 per student/per year, paid by the federal government. Such an amount as a supplemental fund for parents, to cover the cost of private school choice or to be added to the funds available for public school for each such student, would make an enormous difference in most states. In public schools, these funds would then go to each school building, rather than the school district. Thus, the funds would be used where the neediest children were actually located. Congress could and should do this.

Majority Leader Dick Armey has introduced legislation to extend a Cleveland-type voucher program to students from the poorest families in the District of Columbia. There has never been any good reason not to offer choice programs in the District, where educational quality and poverty can arguably be as bad, if not worse, than Cleveland. Charter schools already exist in the District, serving 14 percent of its school children while, 30 empty public school buildings languish in the city's surplus inventory. In 1998, similar legislation was approved by Congress, but was vetoed by President Bill Clinton. In my opinion, choice should not be limited to the poor, but should be available to all District residents.

President George W. Bush is proposing a plan that will provide tax credits to support individual parent choice, up to $2,500 per student. Tax credits have been found constitutionally acceptable since 1983 in the case of *Mueller v. Allen.*

This is a great day in the history of the rights of families to exercise the power described in *Pierce v. Society of Sisters,* namely, to choose the school best for a particular child.

In 1954, the Supreme Court removed race as a barrier to equal educational opportunity. In 2002, the Court removed poverty as a barrier to equal educational opportunity. *Zelman v. Simmons-Harris* is often described as the great civil rights debate of the twenty first century, as was *Brown v. Board of Education* in the twentieth century. I believe that is a fair comparison.

Bert Holt calls the Cleveland Voucher Plan "The unique emancipating educational opportunity for the urban poor." Empowering the urban poor is the best way to pull them out of poverty and into the middle class. Empowering all urban residents to control the educational environment for their children is the surest way to restore America's cities.

Appendix A.

The Ohio Commission on Educational Choice, 1992

Sharon Bennett (Fremont)
John W. Berry (Dayton)
David Brennan, Chair (Akron)
Ron Budzik (Dayton)
L. Clifford Craig (Cincinnati)
Jean R. Droste (Columbus)
Bruce Feldman (Dayton)
Dr. Lucille G. Ford (Ashland)
Rev. Ronald J. Fowler (Akron)
Dr. Stephen T. House (Dayton)
Arthur Kobacker (Columbus)
Allan Krulak (Cleveland)
William G. Lyden (Youngstown)
Robert W. Mahoney (North Canton)
John McConnell (Columbus)
Harold McMaster (Perrysburg)
Samuel Miller (Cleveland)
Dennis Minshall (Columbus)
Pat Mitchell (Cuyahoga Falls)
Thomas Noe (Sylvania)
Jack Partridge (Cincinnati)
Joseph A. Pichler (Cincinnati)
Burnell Roberts (Dayton)
Dr. Richard Ross (Reynoldsburg)
Ralph Schey (Westlake)
Dr. Steve Scovic (Fairborn)
Stan Sobel (Belmont)
Charles Taylor (Cleveland)
Harry Winch (Minster)

Appendix B.

	VOUCHERS PRIVATE	CHARTERS PUBLIC
Legal Entity	All Types	Not for Profit Corporation
Permanence	Indefinite	Usually 5 years
Accountability	Consumer Choice	Charter Conditions Consumer Choice
Open Records Law	No	Usually required
Channel	Through Parent	Directly to the School
Amount	Usually somewhat less than charter, but not necessarily	Generally 60%-90% of public per student
Start Up Grants	No	Federal @ $450M/School
Teachers	Need not be certified	Usually, teachers must be certified
Unions	Possible per school	Possible per school
State Control	Minimal	As required by statute; more than minimal
For Profit	Can be	Usually not
Religious	Can be	Cannot be
NLRB Jurisdiction	Only if non-religious	Yes
Transportation Provided	Usually	Usually
Time to first open school	As little as 90 days	Usually 12-24 months

Appendix C.

A Synopsis of Legal Challenges to the Ohio School Choice Plan

June 1995   The Ohio General Assembly enacts the plan.

January 1996   The American Federation of Teachers challenges the plan in state court.

May 1999   The Ohio Supreme Court declares the plan unconstitutional on procedural grounds (the so-called "single issue rule"), but constitutional on First Amendment grounds. The Ohio Legislature immediately re-passes the legislation in a free-standing bill. The American Civil Liberties Union and the teachers' unions file a similar suit in federal court.

August 1999   Federal Judge Solomon Oliver rules that the plan cannot continue while being litigated; then partially rescinds his decision, allowing all but new students to remain in the program another year.

November 1999   In an unprecedented decision, the United States Supreme Court lifts the injunction.

December 2000   A three-judge panel of the Sixth Circuit Court of Appeals rules 2-1 against the plan. Ohio Attorney General Betty Montgomery appeals the decision to the United States Supreme Court.

September 2001   The Supreme Court agrees to hear the appeal.

February 2002   The Supreme Court hears oral arguments.

June 27, 2002   Decision—the United States Supreme Court reverses the judgment of the Court of Appeals.

Appendix D.

IN THE UNITED STATES DISTRICT COURT
FOR THE NORTHERN DISTRICT OF OHIO
EASTERN DIVISION

DORIS SIMMONS-HARRIS, et al.,	CASE NO. 1:99 CV 1740
Plaintiffs,	JUDGE SOLOMON
vs.	OLIVER, JR.
DR. SUSAN TAVE ZELMAN Defendant.	
SUE GATTON, et al.,	CASE NO. 1:99 CV 1818
Plaintiffs	
vs.	
DR. SUSAN TAVE ZELMAN, et al.,	
Defendant	

AFFIDAVIT OF DAVID L. BRENNAN

In the State of Ohio: ss
County of Summit   :

Being first duly cautioned and sworn, David L. Brennan says and deposes that he has personal knowledge of the following:

1. Affiant is a lifelong resident of Akron, Ohio, an attorney for 40 years, and over the last 25 years has been CEO of numerous manufacturing companies, employing over 5,000 people.

2. The manufacturing companies owned and operated by Affiant since 1975 are in traditional manufacturing industries, such as steel, stampings, plastics, and various fabricated parts. Because of the functional illiteracy and innumeracy of over half of the production employees in these companies, learning centers were established for the purpose of providing basic educational skills to employees. The programs were very successful utilizing computer-based instruction. Affiant attempted to involve the existing public school system using these techniques, to no avail. When scholarship/voucher and community/charter schools became available, this was the first opportunity to pursue education techniques which had been so successful for the company employees.

3. In 1998-99, HOPE Tremont Academy and HOPE Central Academy were two operating private schools, grades K-5. Students were funded under

153

the Cleveland Scholarship and Tutoring Program (CSTP). In the spring of 1999, the Ohio Supreme Court had not yet decided about the constitutionality of the CSTP. Our parents were very anxious about the existence of the schools for their children in September 1999. After consultation with the parents, it was decided to close the two voucher supported schools as of June 30, 1999, which was done. Two new community schools were formed to take over the premises as of July 1, 1999. Thus, the former students had the option of applying to other participating scholarship schools, or applying to new community schools to be opened on the same premises. Many parents who previously sent their children to the two scholarship schools decided to enroll their children in the new community schools.

4. In order to attract students to our Cleveland Scholarship and Tutoring Program schools, only those students holding a scholarship were eligible to attend, and we competed with the other 54 schools in the program for these students. In 1996, 350 parents chose to send their children to our two new academies.

5. In order to attract students to our community schools, we engaged in newspaper and radio advertising, flyers, organization meetings, and the

like. Further, we had teams of 6-8 people who went out into the neighborhoods surrounding our schools acquainting our neighbors with the availability of the school. All of our schools start with waiting lists for most of the classes.

6. Our community schools are in competition with all other schools in Cleveland. We compete with the Cleveland Municipal School District, traditional and magnet schools, and with other community schools located in Cleveland. A parent dissatisfied with the education offered at one of our community schools can easily choose one of the other available alternatives.

7. This competitive environment forces us to do our best to deliver high quality effective education to our students. Our typical classroom has a teacher, and a part-time or full-time aid, together with six computers, utilizing fully integrated software, with Internet access.

8. I have been involved with the organization of 11 community schools in Ohio. There is a significant demand by parents for an alternative to the local public school system. Educational entrepreneurs like me stand ready to meet this demand. To the extent the current demand exceeds current supply, additional facilities will be built.

9. As the community school program grows, there should be no shortage of community schools, if the State Board of Education continues to approve the applications without additional regulatory requirements. The current level of $4,500 per student is adequate to start a comprehensive and effective school.

10. It has been my experience that the parents who sent their children to the two HOPE scholarship schools, as well as the parents who currently send their children to the community schools, are sophisticated educational consumers. They explore all the options and choose a school based upon what they believe is best for their children. Parents who choose a scholarship school, rather than a community school, make this choice because, from their perspective, that choice is a better option. The same can be said for parents who make the opposite choice.

FURTHER AFFIANT SAYETH NAUGHT.

/s/   David L. Brennan
DAVID L. BRENNAN

Sworn to before me and subscribed in my presence this 26 day of October, 1999.

NOTARY PUBLIC

Acknowledgement

The authors thank the *Alexis de Tocqueville Institution* and Chairman Gregory Fossedal for invaluable assistance in making this book possible. Prior to the U.S. Supreme Court's historic decision in *Zelman v. Simmons-Harris* on June 27, 2002, the Institution published "The Cleveland Voucher Case," an advanced edition of the first section of this book. In particular, it provided background to the media in covering the Supreme Court's ruling. The *Alexis de Tocqueville Institution* (www.adti.net) studies the extension and perfection of democracy. It places special emphasis on original journalistic scholarship as a critical means of achieving this mission. Like de Tocqueville himself, the institution is non-partisan and adheres to the ideals of political equality, civil liberty, and economic initiative.